"The Spirit of '76"

..... an American Portrait

"The Spirit of '76"

..... an American Portrait

America's Best Known Painting, Least Known Artist

By Willard F. Gordon

Distributed by
QUAIL HILL ASSOCIATES
Box 1776
Fallbrook, California
92028

(By golly, this ought to make them take note!)

SKETCH—A.M.WILLARD.   The Sketch Book 1883

Impish boy on stool (A-81)
(Cleveland Public Library)

TABLE OF CONTENTS

PREFACE

With the Bicentennial year of 1976, there is an increasing interest in the American artist, Archibald M. Willard, and his famous patriotic painting, The **Spirit of '76**, or as he preferred to title it, **Yankee Doodle.**

The painting received popular recognition at The Centennial Exposition in Philadelphia in 1876, and has been seen by generations of Americans, making it one of the best known and frequently copied of our Nation's paintings.

Willard was a homespun, self-trained, physical giant of a man, who had a never-ending compulsion to express himself with pen or brush. From simple artistic beginnings as a wagon painter in his home town of Wellington, Ohio, he received prominence in his lifetime as an artist in the Cleveland area.

Although best known for his patriotic works, Willard excelled at humor, deriving most of his income from the sale of humorous chromolithographs published by his friend and promoter, J. F. Ryder. Willard's Americana themes incorporated serious or touching issues appropriate to the times. Additionally, the development of portraiture and landscapes span his lifetime. Many of these early works are collector's items in themselves for their primitive style.

Willard was quite versatile, creating many hundreds of different works, in pencil, crayon, oil and pastel. He painted not only on paper and canvas, but on most any surface that would sustain his artistic endeavors. None of the original wagons remain, but fortunately many of his canvases are reappearing—predominantly in the northern Ohio area. Additionally, his works include murals, book illustrations, and reportedly some sculpture.

Willard often repeated his favorite works, which became quite an enigma, not only in **The Spirit of '76** but also in many other paintings. He often personally modeled for dramatic themes and his face appears in several group paintings. A small number of his works were signed, even fewer dated.

As a great-great-nephew of the artist, I have spent a number of years attempting to locate and catalog his works and compile a comprehensive research document on the artist. This book is divided into five parts— the story of **The Spirit of '76**, the controversial story of the "Spirit(s) of '76," a biography of the artist emphasizing specific works, a section on lost paintings, and a Catalogue Raisonné of Willard's total effort.

Willard has not been recognized by the 'authorities' on American Art. Perhaps this has just been an oversight due to the heretofore non-availability of data on the man and his works.

But then, on the other hand, the age-old question remains—What is Art? What constitutes sufficient merit to warrant fame and recognition?

Willard's obituary best sums up the contribution of this one artist to the American scene . . .

> "It may be that the late A. M. Willard was not a great painter. He lacked training; he lacked opportunities, but his work was filled with an inspiration that overshadowed technical skill. His one great effort—great in originality, in sincerity, in heart appeal, stood out among American paintings, . . . It became the best known picture in our country . . ."[66]

Yet I hate to think that this one isolated work is all that Willard should be remembered for. The following pages will attest to a genius of sorts—an artist who, although lacking in classic technique, was a master in plucking the heart strings of a Nation.

So that a great Country may know one of its truly significant artist—this effort is directed . . .

ACKNOWLEDGEMENTS

Little in Willard's original hand remains. We are indebted to J. F. Ryder for his autobiography "Voigtlander and I" and for his "The Painter of Yankee Doodle," **New Englander Magazine**, December, 1895. Reverend William Barton, the artist's friend, provided us with several magazine articles—"The Painter of Yankee Doodle," **Success**, July, 1898, and "America's Most Popular Patriotic Picture," **Ladies Home Journal**, April, 1919. Additionally, there was an important exchange of letters between these two gentlemen in the 1890's.

Important first person interviews with Willard were printed in **Everybody's Magazine**, July, 1917, **The Housekeeper**, July, 1912, and the various Cleveland newspapers during the artist's life span. We are dependent upon their journalistic integrity.

One final basic document is the book, "The Spirit of '76" by the young drummer boy, Henry K. Devereux, privately printed in 1926.

I am indebted to many others for their original research, but must singularly acknowledge the master's thesis of Arthur H. Auten, Western Reserve University, Cleveland, 1960. His extensive research and bibliography provided a wealth of background information upon which to build.

I also wish to acknowledge the series on Willard by the Wellington historian, Robert L. Walden, appearing in the Wellington Enterprise in the mid 1950's, from which I borrowed most liberally.

I must most gratefully acknowledge the interest, encouragement and many courtesies extended to me on behalf of "Uncle Arch."

To my mother, Marjorie, who was first a Willard; to my cousin Marjorie, who started me on a family quest —

To Jane Rosequist and Dick Reilly, who helped to make our personal **Spirit of '76** dream a reality —

To my many kinfolk in the Willard Family Association, especially Elsie and Stephen F. — To William McChesney of the Mosher Clan —

In the Cleveland Area: To Lee Wachtel, former librarian Cleveland City Hall; The Fine Arts Department of the Cleveland Public Library; The staff of the Western Reserve Historical Society for years of help and understanding, with special thanks to Jack Large and Kermit Pike; To the Vixseboxse Galleries; To Mr. Alden Hare —

To Dick Squire of the Bedford Historical Society; to B. E. Kelley of the Fayette Co. Historical Society; and to Margaret Ford of the Geauga Co. Historical Society.

To the whole wonderful town of Wellington, Ohio, with special recognition to Ernie Henes and the Southern Lorain Co. Historical Society, to Ray and Kathy LaMacchia, Pat Lindley, Ted & Betty Thoms, Ed & Maxine Wells, and Virginia Willard. To former Wellingtonian, Prof. Robert Gregg.

To two ladies in Marblehead for encouraging me to "more sufficiently prepare" the story of the **Marblehead Spirit of '76**.

To the Shillito/Rob Paris Studios, Cincinnati, Ohio.

To the Diamond Shamrock Corporation for sponsoring exhibitions of Willard Art; to Niles Varney, New*Spirit/Wellington Willard Art Exhibition Director.

To Joanna and the kids -

And finally I would be quite remiss if I did not acknowledge the special efforts of my typist June Prentice, and my publisher, Ernie Gentle and the staff of Aero Publishers, with special thanks to Jan, Mike and Dora, not only for their professional expertise, but also for a personal concern beyond the call of duty.

FOREWORD

I am most fortunate in obtaining the counsel of several distinguished Willard authorities in creating a comprehensive FOREWORD to the book — Their sentiments constitute a fitting testimonial to the artist. I only wish sufficient space were available to print their comments in entirety . . .

Willard F. Gordon
Quail Hill Ranch
Box 1776
Fallbrook, California
92028

* * * * * * * *

Foreword by Robert D. Gregg . . .

Archibald Willard was born, reared, and spent most of his life in the Western Reserve region of Ohio. This area derived its name from the fact that its lands were awarded to New England Revolutionary War veterans, since the new, struggling Federal Government did not have sufficient funds to pay them for their wartime services. The marks of this new region show in Willard's life—a fervent patriotism, an innovative spirit, and a frontier feeling of class and race equality, including deep seated abolitionism.

Willard's patriotism is embodied particularly in his greatest painting, "The Spirit of '76." This painting, with its three heroic Revolutionary War figures marching into battle, has probably reached into more homes and hearts in this country than any American painting ever produced. It is a kind of "Battle Hymn of the Republic" on canvas. The painting crops up repeatedly in hundreds of books, in large tableaux, in pageants, and in firework displays. Even as the artist applied his brush, long seasoning experience guided his hand. From his first ancestor in this country, Major Simon Willard, who came to the Massachusetts Bay Colony in 1634 and was one of the founders of Concord, one generation after another served to develop the artist's insight. A particularly strong influence was his grandfather who was a relative of General Stark and who was with him in the campaign against General Burgoyne, which ended with the British surrender at Saratoga in one of the most decisive phases of the Revolution. Above all, Archibald's patriotism was tempered in the experience of his own long, hard four years' service in the Civil War. On the innovative side, Willard's work shows the flexible, untrammeled spirit of a new country.

In regard to the spirit of equality, the Western Reserve was a fervent center of abolitionism in the days before the Civil War. When Willard was growing up in Wellington, it was an important station on the "Underground Railway," spiriting escaped slaves from the South to Canada. As a matter of fact, Wellington was the site of the famous Oberlin-Wellington Rescue Case in which a slave was forcibly taken by townspeople from the owner and United States marshals. James Ford Rhodes, in his authoritative "History of the United States Since the Compromise of 1850" calls this one of the most important incidents hastening the Civil War.

Thus, Archibald Willard, like all of us, was a product of his own region and his own times. His love of country runs deep, as evidenced particularly in his great masterpiece of which about fifteen "originals" are known to exist. His innovative qualities, and his regard for fair play for men of all races and social and economic conditions marked him as a man of character and good judgment. His work was a great contribution to the Centennial of 1876 and continues to be such in the Bicentennial of 1976.

Robert D. Gregg
Dean, College of Liberal Arts, and Professor of History Emeritus,
Willamette University, Salem, Oregon

Foreword by Edward S. Wells . . .

Physical science tells us that a releasing force is not proportional to the force released. More than a century ago this law of physics was demonstrated by the artist, Archibald M. Willard. As a youth he arrived with his family in Wellington where his budding talent as a painter led to his first job, that of a striper of carriages. The stripes grew into scrolls and flowers and even simple scenes as he became more skilled and confident. Away from his work he continued to wield his brush, using furniture and walls as his canvas along with paper and wood.

Wellington's traditional Fourth of July parade and celebration, which young Willard had witnessed annually, furnished him a magnificent opportunity to delineate the scenes his mind's eye had recorded. He was caught up in the exhileration and patriotic fever the holiday engendered.

Willard's initial portrayal was a cartoon-like picture of the parade musicians, which he entitled "Yankee Doodle." The releasing force of the inspiration drawn from the Fourth of July holiday was expanded many fold as the painter refined his early sketches of Yankee Doodle to express more accurately the message he wanted his viewers to get. He altered the actions of his figures until the theme was a serious expression of stirring patriotic feeling. With its altered appearance and serious message came a new name—The Spirit of '76.

Friends who dropped in on Willard as he labored to get just the right expression or correct movement offered occasional suggestions and considerable encouragement. A photographer friend made a series of photographs of the models which greatly aided in capturing the facial expressions Willard sought. Helpful as all these were, they in no way distracted him from his central idea.

Wellington is tremendously proud that it could furnish the releasing force that a simple small town holiday produced. It is likewise proud that Archibald Willard held the town in high regard. He had not been able to choose his birthplace, but he did select Wellington as the place where he was to be buried.

Edward S. Wells
Wellington, Ohio

* * * * * * * *

Foreword by Ray La Macchia . . .

The Spirit of '76 — An American Portrait. I can already hear those wise sages saying "trite," "mediocre," "ho-hum!" But then how do they account for the almost inaudible rumble throughout our land that keeps recalling grandma's apple pie and the flag. It **really is** an American portrait! What is there about the painting that we continue to carve it in wood, etch it in stone, hammer it on bronze, photograph it, restyle it, caricature it? I think it is a mirror image of what Americans want to see in themselves—An American Portrait.

But what of the artist, Archibald Willard? What of his life, his other works, his impact on the art community?

I can only judge him by comments from the thousands of "common Americans" across the country who have seen some of his other works in our Wellington Collection Exhibit. The eye of the beholder has spoken. Willard has indeed made a significant contribution recalled with even greater impact in this troubled Bicentennial year. His contribution is to help us remember old tradition, new spirit and new hope.

Ray La Macchia
President - NewSpirit/Wellington

Foreword by Ernst L. Henes . . .

In 1876 our nation noted its Centennial at Philadelphia. Among the varied exhibitions was an acre and a half of art including Europe's masterpieces, yet the hundreds of thousands who came to admire were entranced with Archibald M. Willard's "Spirit of '76." As a result, the heretofore unknown artist won immediate acclaim.

It is now 1976, the nation is observing its Bicentennial, and "Uncle Arch," as he became known by relatives and friends, is being re-acclaimed in every city and hamlet across the land.

A full century has elapsed since this self-taught artist captured the spirit that brought us our independence and placed it on canvas to become America's most inspirational patriotic work of art.

As a result, the "Spirit of '76" has become known to every adult American, pupils in every school in the land, plus millions of folks throughout the world. But it is Wellington, Ohio, the artist's home town, that reveres his memory most, owns the largest collection of his works, and has paid him tribute in numerous ways.

It was here that the artist conceived the idea for his masterpiece; where three of the four persons portrayed by him in it were chosen for their respective roles, where he chose his wife and where he chose to be buried.

As a result, Wellington's Public Square has become Willard Memorial Square; its museum has become the "Spirit of '76" Museum; the village monument erected to honor Wellingtonians who gave their lives in all our nation's wars bears the design of his famous "Spirit."

Wellington is a little town with a big story—thanks to "Uncle Arch." Naturally, all of us who live here are more Willard conscious than ever before. He stirred the hearts of Americans and we are proud to be a part of his community; to trod the same streets that he walked: to view the scenes that he saw and which inspired him to produce so great a masterpiece.

Ernst L. Henes, President
Southern Lorain Co. Historical Society and Director of The "Spirit of '76" Museum

* * * * * * * *

Foreword by Richard J. Squire . . .

Archibald Willard's increasingly familiar creation of a century ago has become the symbol of the bicentennial. Two men and a boy have been marching through America for more than a century. Two drummers and a fifer have brought the spirit of freedom throughout our land. The inspirational vision of the three Revolutionary War figures striding along in the battle for independence has become familiar to millions of Americans in the past ten decades.

Here at the Bedford Historical Society museum we have a large file on Archibald Willard and the "Spirit of '76," as well as numerous Willard lithographs and other related items. The Willard birthplace home is just a block away.

Now, between the covers of this book, we finally have a rich concentration of facts about our favorite painter and his masterpiece. Here we find a wealth of information that may be found nowhere else in print.

It is particularly noteworthy that this publication about the "Spirit of '76" and its creator appear in the year of our nation's bicentennial and the year of the painting's centennial.

Richard J. Squire
Bedford Historical Society
Bedford, Ohio

REFERENCES

Ryder, James F., **Voigtlander & I In Pursuit of Shadow Catching**, Cleveland: The Imperial Press, 1902
#45, p. 216-217; #46, p. 218; #49, p. 228; #50, p. 223-224

Ryder, James F. "The Painter of Yankee Doodle," **New England Magazine** XIII (Dec. 1895)
#1, p. 492; #6, p. 488; #9, p. 487; #15, p. 494; #48, p. 485; #52, p. 487

Kennedy, James H., "Yankee Doodle in Paint," **Everybody's Magazine** (July 1917)
#3, p. 14; #31, p. 15; #33, p. 15-16; #35, p. 16

Willard, A.M., "The Picture That Would Not Be Funny," **The Housekeeper** (July 1912)
#29, p. 5; also nos. 30, 32, 36, 38, and 42 and 43
#4, p. 6; also nos. 8, 10, 11, 14, and 47

Devereux, Henry K., **The Spirit of '76**, Cleveland, Arthur H. Clark Company, 1926
#5, p. 53-55; #7, p. 42-44; #17, p. 55-57; #18, p. 77; #19, p. 74; #22, "Illustrations;" #25, p. 78; #26, p. 74-75

"Willard's Talk," **Cleveland Town Topics**, XLII (1912) #2, #12, #13, #20

The Sketch Book, Cleveland Academy of Art (1883-1884)
#34, #39, #59, #60

Letters: Ryder to Barton (Oct. 25 & Dec. 14, 1895), Herrick Memorial Library, Wellington, Ohio, #23

Cleveland Plain Dealer, Cle. June 12, 1932, #24

Wellington Enterprise:
  June 21, 1916, #37
  Walden, Robert L., "The Willard Story"
    #28, ch. 21; #40, ch. 17; #41, ch. 2; #65, ch. 21; #67, ch. 19, #68, ch. 20
  Willard, Virginia, June 27, 1968, #44

Cleveland Leader:
  March 28, 1876, p. 7, #53
  January 10, 1877, p. 7, #54
  Dec. 15, 1881, p. 5, #57
  Nov. 23, 1882, p. 4, #58
  Aug. 25, 1901, p. 26, #62 & #64

Cleveland Herald:
  March 27, 1877, p. 8, #55
  Oct. 16, 1877, p. 4, #56
  Aug. 30, 1878, p. 8, #16
  Aug. 26, 1878, p. 8, #63
  Nov. 13, 1878, p. 7, #61

Elyria Chronicle Telegram, June 22, 1931, p. 7, #66

Boston Herald, October 20, 1898, #21

Painting Ownership & Photographic Credit Codes

W.R.H.S. — Western Reserve Historical Society, Cleveland, Ohio
H.M.L. — Herrick Memorial Library, Wellington, Ohio
S.L.C.H.S. — Southern Lorain Co. Historical Society, Wellington, Ohio
W.F.G. — Photographs by the author

J. F. RYDER - 1876

Despite the snow flurries and March winds that blew from the cold waters of Lake Erie, a sizeable crowd milled on the sidewalk in front of J. F. Ryder's art studio throughout most of the day. Cleveland's most famous photographer and art entrepreneur was quite pleased with the public reaction to the large painting displayed in his front window. After all, it was **he** who

J. F. Ryder
"Voigtlander & I"

Etching by M. E. Heiss
J. F. Ryder Studio

first recognized the talent of the young wagon painter, "Arch" Willard from Wellington. It was **he** who brought Willard to Cleveland where they developed a profitable partnership printing chromolithographs of Willard's humorous sketches. In fact, it was **he** who suggested to Willard the theme of this giant canvas.

Ryder tells of the public reaction to the painting:

"The crowds which gathered about it blockaded the entrance to the gallery and obstructed the sidewalk to such an extent that it was necessary to remove it from the window to the rear of the store, where it was on exhibition for several days, during which

time all business in the store was discontinued on account of the crowds which filled the place. The interest and enthusiasm which it created were remarkable."[1]

J. F. Ryder Studio

J. F. Ryder
(H.M.L.)

J. F. Ryder was well prepared to promote this new work of art. With the Centennial Exhibition in Philadelphia only three months away, the presses were already rolling out chromos of Willard's new **Yankee Doodle**. Ryder's news release for the Monday morning, March 29th edition of the "Cleveland Leader" was a tribute to his promotional genius. It has been quoted and paraphrased many times since then.

YANKEE DOODLE
Willard's Grand Centennial Painting

"Were the Centennial Exposition to be entirely unsupplied with music, the lack would almost be filled by placing Willard's **Yankee Doodle** where it could meet the glance of every American visitor, for but a glance at it is needed to set all the fires of patriotism burning in one's veins, and to compel his footsteps to keep time to the music which he **feels** if he does not hear—for every line in the picture equals a drum tap, and every color thrills like the shrill martial note of the fife. The artist has seized a moment when all artificialities fall from a man's soul, as the cumbersome baggage falls from his shoulders,—in that supreme moment when he leads or is led into battle. The three main figures which have been sketched upon the canvas meet all the requirements of the situation, and are in keeping with the surroundings. Over them the clouds of smoke lower, dimming the red and blue of the flag which waves behind them and marks the line of the advancing column, where a few brave Continentals struggle up the perilous height. At their feet is a dismantled cannon, on the ruins of which a dead soldier lies, his peaceful sleep in sad contrast to the motion and action all about him.

"But the picture itself lies in the center, where the trio of homespun musicians are furnishing, with all their might and power, that music which has been since 'heard round the world,' and whose shrill melody is so full of patriotism that it is, and always will be, the Grand National Tune of America—glorious, grand old 'Yankee Doodle!' The old drummer who walks in the

in the air and his eyes set clear and defiant as though he saw the danger but feared it not, with the sharp curves around his mouth drawn to a set determination which is not angry defiance, but heroic resistance—all these combine to make up that wonderful figure in history which no rags could degrade nor spendor make nobler—the Continental soldier! The face is rugged and hard, but in it one sees that heroism and endurance which made 1776 stand out, forever prominent among the great years of history.

W.F.G.

Thomas Gift (SP-9) 1912
(Metromedia, Inc.)

"On the left of the old drummer is the fifer, whose calm, collected face wears a look as full of heroism, but of a far simpler and more patient kind, than that of the other. The man seems to have come there for one object—to blow his fife; and that he will do as well, here in the shower of bullets, as though at the porch of his cottage. His eyes are fixed toward the sky as though reading the notes of his music on the clouds. His bloody handkerchief around his brow tells of the bullet that came so near, but spared him for the work in hand. His blue coat, buttoned to the chin, is neat and orderly, and he seems to have left all direction and guidance to his companion, so that he could pour his whole force and energy into the reed at his lips. And how he does blow! It seems almost as though one could hear the shrill notes, as he goes marching on over the broken cannon and dead soldier—raising 'Yankee Doodle' above the clamor and noise of battle.

"On the right of the old drummer marches a boy—hardly in his teens—as clean and

City of Cleveland

Cleveland Commission (SP-10) 1913
(Cleveland City Hall)

center, bare headed, grand in his fearlessness, with his coat thrown off and his back as straight as though the years were not piled so thick upon it, with one sleeve rolled up as though he had thrown down the spade to grasp the drumsticks, his white hair blown

Devereux's Purchase (SP-7) 1877/1892
(Abbot Hall, Marblehead, Mass.)

THE ARTIST

Willard himself was also pleased with the public reaction to **Yankee Doodle**. More important, he was relieved that the large 8'x10' canvas was finished. He was exhausted from several months of arduous labor. What had started as a humorous cartoon, a promotion for the Centennial, had evolved into an emotional and totally consuming experience for Willard. He had truly captured the spirit of those early American patriots of 1776.

It should have been a time of great joy for the artist, but his heart was heavy from the recent death of his father, Reverend Samuel R. Willard, who not only modeled for the grey-haired old drummer, but inspired the transformation of the painting and symbolized its message.

_W.F.G.

Self Portrait II (P-2) Circa 1876   (W.R.H.S.)
Willard about the time he painted the "Spirit of '76"

sweet as though just kissed by his mother before the daily run to school. His drum keeps time to the music of the other, and his face is upturned to the old man—perhaps his grandfather—as though to question the route or the danger. But he never falters, and no shade of fear lurks in those open eyes, while the 'rub-a-dub' of his little drum seems to sound as clear and distinct as the shrill notes of the fife or the heavier roll of the heavier drummer.

"It is a picture worth seeing—in itself an embodiment of the hardships of the Revolution. Its conception is wonderful, and its execution a crown of honor to the painter. It is a story which tells itself at a glance, and has been told as truthfully and poetically as art could tell it. To have wrought so great a work proclaims Willard as one on whom genius has placed her hand, and the city should be proud that he had made it his home. The critic who views it merely as a work of art may possibly find flaws in the execution, but the American who looks upon it and remembers Bunker Hill, will recognize that he has found a man who could crown the Centennial year with a grand artistic triumph. 'Yankee Doodle' has been glorified in art as it never was before.

"There is much more that could be said with pleasure, but it is not needed. The picture itself will tell its own story, and is more eloquent than words. It will remain at Ryder's for a few days longer, where all can see it for themselves."

DEVELOPMENT OF THE YANKEE DOODLE THEME

In several newspaper and magazine articles, Willard gives us a detailed background of the painting.

. . . "In our younger days there were the old militia gatherings of the state. Every able-bodied man of the time was compelled to get out in the summer and to undergo training so that he could be called upon in an emergency. At the time I speak of, the militia had rather degenerated because there were no very stringent laws about calling out the men and there was no rigid discipline, so that the affair resolved itself into an old-fashioned picnic. Wives and children went to the camp, there was martial music, and all had a good time. It was not unusual for men to imbibe a little too freely as they do today. They used a kind of rum as strong in its effect as whiskey. We saw old drummers of the War of 1812 enjoying these social occasions, and as they got a bit excited, marching along in a peculiar high stepping manner. That gave me an idea for the **Yankee Doodle** picture.[2]

A.M.Willard

H.M.L.

Fourth of July Musicians Cartoon (SP-1)
In 1895 Willard recreated his "Yankee Doodle" sketch. The original cartoon, circa 1873, had been discarded. (H.M.L.)

. . . "No uniforms were in evidence, except here and there . . . There were few guns or swords, and only occasionally an outbreak of fuss and feathers. But always the flag, the fife, and drum, the musicians with heads up, and high-stepping of the van of the column . . . . . With the exaggerated or burlesque idea at the fore, I slashed into outline a few charcoal attempts . . ."[3]

"There was a 'Three Finger Dick' who tossed the drumsticks and varied the beat . . . on the chime. I made him my central figure . . . As a fifer, I had . . . a picturesque character, and had in him a vein of fun . . . To balance the fifer, I needed another drummer and took a farmer boy, beating his drum as part of the day's work, too intent on not missing a stroke to feel any particular inspiration . . . I worked for weeks over this humorous picture. At times I almost had it, but just as I was approaching a satisfactory

treatment of the theme, I would feel a strong sense of dissatisfaction, throw away my sketch and begin anew."[4]

THE DRUMMER BOY

On the 6th of March, 1876, young Henry K. Devereux, a student at the Brooks Military Academy, led his Third Company to a decisive victory in a special drill competition to honor the Cleveland Greys. Every boy was determined to impress these old Civil War heroes with their military accomplishment. Somehow, the honors always seemed to be awarded by natural sympathy to the younger boys.

One old veteran in attendance, Archibald M. Willard, was seeking a subject to model for the young drummer boy. Impressed with Devereux's military bearing, the artist received permission from the boy's father to utilize the boy's services as the **Yankee Doodle** model.

Devereux's book, **The Spirit of '76,** published

HENRY KELSEY DEVEREUX
who posed for the drummer boy. From an original portrait taken about 1878
H. K. Devereux
"The Spirit of '76"

in 1926, gives a detailed account of his role in the **Yankee Doodle** story.

"Shortly after this competitive drill, my father told me he had given permission to Mr. Willard to use me as a model for the drummer boy in his picture. I recall a feeling of resentment on my part for that meant giving up afternoon play, a thing not to be contemplated with a feeling of joy by any boy. However, paternal edicts generally prevail, and a beginning was made by going down to Mr. Ryder's gallery and posing for a number of photos. This was followed by a number of visits to Willard's studio where hours were passed in rather a trying way for a boy. Willard was very kind and thoughtful. He entertained me with stories of the war, told me what was in his mind for the creation of this picture, and often would let me rest and walk in front of the picture to see what he had done. I can recall the enthusiasm of the man. He worked as if possessed of an idea that pleased him, but which he might lose. With watching him work and the picture develop, I too soon became enthusiastic. I forgot that it was tiresome to stand on one leg, and that bent, the other advanced, and the foot resting on an inverted box, with the head twisted to one side and the eyes raised and arms outstretched, although it was very exacting of one's temper and strength. However, things progressed rapidly, and by the thirtieth of March the picture was about finished, and I took my mother, at Willard's request, to see it. I am sure she experienced the feeling that thousands of our mothers have when they have seen their beloved son marching off to war. And then the momentous day came when it was rolled up and sent to the Centennial.

"That fall I went to the Centennial with my parents. We spent about two weeks there. Almost every day I went into the Art Gallery to stand before **The Spirit of '76.** Each time I felt something aroused in me that did not diminish by the frequent visits. It also was curious to mark the effect on others. Always there was a crowd in front of the picture and many if not most of the people had perceptible tears arise to their eyes as they stood and gazed. Many actually cried, yet came again and again to look with reverence on that canvas that pulsed so much of American spirit."[5]

THE FIFER

"For the fifer he chose an old farmer soldier who had blown his fife through the wars, its shrill notes bracing the weary legs of the marching soldiers. Brave old Hugh Mosher, who had carried the musket as well as the fife."[6]

So continued the flowery writings of J. F. Ryder. Mosher and Willard were close boyhood friends from the Wellington area. Both had fought in the Civil War, serving in the Ohio Volunteers, Mosher sustaining considerable injuries while serving as a fifer with the 43rd Infantry Regiment. Like Willard, Mosher was a tall man well over six feet in height, but in contrast was rather rugged in appearance. After the War, he returned to his farming, and unfortunately spent considerable time and finances in the fruitless pursuit of an English inheritance, always dreaming and planning for that moment of instant wealth.

Devereux's writings give us further insight into this colorful character.

J. F. Ryder Studio

Hugh Mosher, The Fifer, circa 1875
(H.M.L.)

"He was a celebrated performer on the fife, and his fame had spread throughout the surrounding country. He was probably the best fifer in northern Ohio. It is said of him that he would rather fife than eat. He carried this little instrument with him wherever he went and delighted to play whenever chance offered. No patriotic gathering in or near Wellington was considered complete without Mosher and his fife. He was intensely patriotic, and even in his last illness deeply regretted being unable to attend the celebration of the Fourth of July in his home town of Wellington.

"He spent considerable time posing for Mr. Willard, and many photographs of him

In later life, Mosher became inseparable from his alter ego, and was seldom without fife. Circa 1890's.   (H.M.L.)

THE OLD DRUMMER

The artist, in his own words, best sums up the final development of the **Yankee Doodle** theme.

. . . "My father had the tall strong features I needed and he posed for me with his drum. But just as I seemed to approach a final plan my father was taken sick, and I saw that he was not long to live. Then something of self-condemnation came over me that I had ever treated the theme as a humorous one."[8]

J. F. Ryder further adds to Willard's commentary—

"The extravagant and funny groups would not respond. He could not suit himself. The humorous vein of his crayon was 'off.' The drawings were vigorous, but they were quite lacking in his strong point of fun. At last he felt rebuked at trifling with a subject so serious. He saw that to construe it in a humorous way was out of the question. And now came to him the true spirit of patriotic fire . . . The sketches from now on were endowed with a force and meaning quite lacking in his former effort. He caught his theme with a strong grasp, carrying it through repeated sketches, each improved upon the last until the design was well established."[9]

The Reverend Samuel Willard
who posed for the central figure in the painting

were taken by Mr. William F. Sawtelle, a photographer of Wellington, for use in Willard's painting. Willard, however, could not get satisfactory photographs of Hugh Mosher. This was before the day of the quick-acting shutter. The cap of the camera could not be operated quickly enough to get satisfactory expression. For this reason, poor Hugh Mosher had to go to Willard's studio and pose. In order to get the proper expression, Mosher not only had to pose, but had to continue fifing all the time he was posing. Willard had a habit of calling attention to the peculiar way in which Mosher held his fife—with the thumb out.

"The rumor is that after Willard had made his many and individual studies of Mosher, that Mosher was unable to get to Cleveland to see the finished canvas of **The Spirit of '76.** He did not see it until he visited the Centennial.

"At the Centennial there was always a crowd around the painting. Mosher joined the crowd. While he thus stood before the picture, someone in the crowd recognized him and he was immediately given an ovation."[7]

Reportedly, Hugh Mosher was later summoned to Washington to play at the White House.

Willard continues:

"A certain inspiration came to me. I saw my models, Harry Devereux, a fine manly boy, Hugh Mosher and my father in a new light. I saw them in imagination on the battlefield. I had seen such men there. I looked into my father's face and the lines of the commonplace faded out, and instead I saw the grand old man, then nearing death, a fine, old man whose soldier spirit had been with him in the years of his privation and self-denial. I saw Hugh Mosher as I had seen such men in battle. The whole idea took on new significance. I tied a bandage around the head of Hugh Mosher. I put his fine, manly boyhood into Harry Devereux. And into the old drummer I put, as I saw it, the dignity and fortitude and moral heroism of my father. And now I had to work hard and fast, dividing my time, watching nights with my father and painting by day. My father did not live to see the result. But I finished the painting under the inspiration of his character."[10]

THE FALLEN SOLDIER

When one thinks of the **Spirit of '76**, one immediately envisions those three heroic figures—the old and young drummers, and the fifer. But what of the fourth and often neglected principal figure, the fallen soldier?

In her elderly years, Mrs. Rufus J. Curtis became obsessed with immortalizing the name of her late husband, brother-in-law and neighbor of the artist, as that of the subject for the fallen soldier. She was only partially correct, for the original model was Charles Spicer, an employee of Wm. Sawtelle. He was temporarily replaced by Jay Wooley, and finally Rufus Curtis did the "laying-in" for the main canvas.

THE CENTENNIAL

Willard continues:

"We sold the photographs as we had planned. The Centennial at Philadelphia kept the printing frames in Mr. Ryder's gallery busy. But this was not the real triumph. The painting itself was sent for and exhibited at the Exposition. It was a life-size canvas, and hung on the line and crowds thronged it day after day."[11]

When asked, "Was it not the most popular painting there?" the artist replied,

"Probably with those who did not think about technique—with the plain American people, like those shown in the picture."[12]

One catalog of Art from the Centennial lists #866, **Yankee Doodle**, Willard, A.M., Cleveland. Not to be outdone as an artist in his own right, photographs by J. F. Ryder are also listed for exhibition.

The **Yankee Doodle** was placed on display in Memorial Hall, supposedly separating it from the "real works of art" representing the best talents of Europe as well as America. Perhaps it was a wise move, for unruly crowds soon recognized the large painting—identifying it from Ryder's chromolithographs.

Public interest in American art was further intensified when Hugh Mosher, himself, stepped into view and filled the air with the shrill notes of his fife. On one occasion, apparently due to the crush of the crowd, an elderly woman is reported to have accidentally thrust her umbrella into the painting. Late that night, Willard returned to

H.M.L.

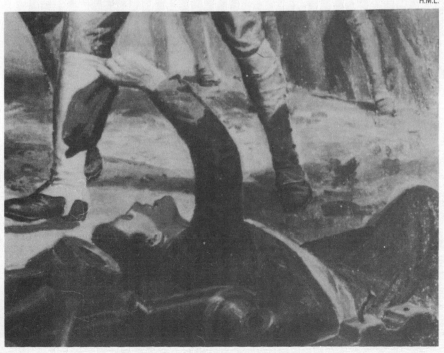

Barton Gift (SP-11) 1916
The Fallen Soldier -
modeled by three
different men.

(H.M.L.)

The most often reproduced early version of "Yankee Doodle"

mend the tear by the light of a lantern and was so absorbed in his work that he failed to note the identity of a solitary figure standing in reverence and awe. It was the President of the United States, Ulysses S. Grant.

ON TO MARBLEHEAD

After the Centennial, the painting was taken to Boston for several weeks where it was placed on exhibition in the Old South Church Meetinghouse. While there, Mr. Brainerd, who had charge of the exhibition, suggested changing the name of the painting from **Yankee Doodle** to **The Spirit of '76** because of the association of the

term Yankee Doodle with a local "half-wit" of the same name. Willard later wrote:

"People got the idea that it was this strange character who was being exhibited."[13]

One Boston writer takes exception to the term "half-wit," inferring that Mr. "Yankee Doodle" was perhaps only just a bit eccentric for he was a cobbler by the name of Issac B. Sawtelle, (no relation to the Wellington photographer.) "Yankee Doodle" made boots, shoes and by way of advertising, while at work or on the street selling, continually whistled or hummed the tune "Yankee Doodle."

Willard, however, reluctantly accepted the new name.

> "I gave it the title which I had first in mind, **Yankee Doodle**. That's the tune I hear when I look at it. But many of those who love it prefer **The Spirit of '76**, and I am content with either."[14]

For the next several years a large **Spirit of '76** toured the country, as Ryder tells us,

> ". . . always by request—so great was the desire of the public to see the painting."[15]

There is considerable controversy as to the actual itinerary; however, included were San Francisco, Chicago, a return trip to Boston, and possibly two trips to Washington, D.C. During the second Boston exhibition, several attempts were made to get better photographs of the painting—one attempt made on the roof of the studio of Messgr. Allen & Rowell.

> "The great size of the picture unfortunately defeated the attempt. It proved too large to be copied."[16]

The records at the Corcoran Galleries in Washington show a painting **Yankee Doodle** was deposited there on February 14, 1879, and removed on May 6, 1880. It was here that General John H. Devereux, railroad executive, financier, philanthropist, and father of the young drummer boy, purchased the painting from Willard for a reported sum of $3,500. He donated it to his home town of Marblehead, Massachusetts, where it is on permanent display in the town meeting hall, Abbot Hall.

Devereux best sums up the significance of the **Spirit of '76** story.

> "Later in life I stood before the picture again . . . Then, as before, not only to me but to all in the room, arose a feeling of sentiment, a feeling of reverence, a feeling almost of awe that made one instinctively bare one's head and swallow the lump that will sometimes come in one's throat.
>
> "It may be that enthusiasm borne of an intimate knowledge of the creation of this picture makes me overenthusiastic, but then and afterwards, even to this day, when I learn how it holds the interest of all that look at it, the belief is strengthened that the picture was an inspiration, though it might be judged crude in execution by artistic standards. I know little or nothing of art, nor does the ordinary individual looking at a picture, but any one picture that can so universally move the onlooker must convey something deeper than the pigments on the canvas."[17]

Bicentennial Commemorative postage stamp of the **"Spirit of '76"** issued January 1, 1976.

Centennial Lithograph
1875 (Library of Congress)

Centennial Photograph
1876 (Litchman)

Devereux Purchase
Marblehead (SP-7)
1877/1892 (U.S. Postal Service)

Western Reserve Hist. Soc.
(Ryder's Gift) (SP-8)
1895 (W.R.H.S.)

Cleveland Commission
(SP-10)
1913 (City of Cleveland)

Thomas Gift (SP-9)
Metromedia
1912 (W.F.G.)

Barton's Gift (SP-11)
Herrick Memorial Library
1916 (W.F.G.)

Comparison of three principal figures in Willard's **Spirit of '76** replicas.

22

CHAPTER II

The Spirit(s) of '76

The **Spirit of '76** is one of the most often parodied and frequently copied of American paintings. Willard himself complicated matters by creating a number of **Spirit(s) of '76**. Unfortunately, he left no records to identify any of his works.

Over the years, there have been two major areas of controversy—which is the original **Spirit of '76**?—and how many of these paintings did he create?

For the sake of analysis, I have divided the **Spirit(s) of '76** into the following categories:

1. Preliminary sketches
2. Early oils
3. Advanced sketches
4. Later oils
5. Water colors
6. Lithographs
7. Signed hand colored photos and lithographs
8. Associated works
9. Fact or fiction

1. PRELIMINARY SKETCHES

Fourth of July Musicians
The very first **Yankee Doodle** or **Spirit of '76** was undoubtedly the **Fourth of July Musicians** cartoon. It was created about 1873 in response to Ryder's suggestion that Willard prepare a marketable chromolithograph for the Centennial. Unfortunately, it has long since disappeared, but at the request of Reverend William Barton, a long time friend of the artist, Willard recreated the cartoon in 1895. The artist called it "The first sketch that was made last."[18] Measuring 13½" by 17½", it is the property of Herrick Memorial Library in Wellington.

Design For a Painting, Copyright
Another important sketch, entitled "Design For a Painting," was filed with the Library of Congress copyright office on October 27, 1875 by J. F. Ryder. (Congressional Library #11242) On the left side of this design are the words "Yankee Doodle" and on the right side the words "J. F. Ryder, Proprietor." This sketch is different from all other renderings of **Yankee Doodle** in that it is proportionately longer widthwise than in height.

Charcoal Sketch
As Willard wrestled with the serious concept of

Diamond Shamrock Corp.

Preliminary Sketch (SP-2) circa 1875   (H.M.L.)
One of the final stages in the evolution of "Yankee Doodle". Believed to be the only study sketch now in existence.

the **Yankee Doodle** theme, many sketches were created and destroyed. Only one of these drawings remains. It, too, is the property of Herrick Memorial Library in Wellington. This charcoal sketch measures 18" by 24" and according to Devereux,

> "This original rough sketch embodies essentially the ideas wrought out in the oil painting, but naturally it is rough and unfinished. The drummer boy is a head shorter. His face is in the shadow. The dying man is much too prominent in the foreground, a mistake which Willard later corrected. Apart from these points, it lacks altogether the spirit and inspiration which Willard worked into his finished painting."[19]

2. EARLY OILS

The First Small Canvas
In Willard's own words,

This small canvas (left) (SP-3) may well be the one Willard painted for the chromo-lithograph in 1875. If so, it is the earliest oil in existence. It is nearly identical in size and composition to the Centennial Lithograph (right) produced in Buffalo, N.Y., by Clay, Cosack & Co. It was in the Buffalo area that the small oil was recently located.

"The first **Yankee Doodle** canvas was the regulation chromo size"[20] . . . "a small one which was reproduced in chromo."[21]

A chromo measuring 18" by 24" and bearing the imprint of "**Yankee Doodle**, 1876, published by J. F. Ryder, Cleveland, Ohio," was printed by Ryder for the Centennial in 1876. It is interesting to note that a small canvas 25¼" by 19¼", not signed or dated, but matching the Ryder lithograph, has recently come to light. Unfortunately, at this time, it has no traceable history to substantiate its authenticity.

The Centennial Original

In October, 1875, Willard began work on the large 8' by 10' canvas in an upstairs bedroom of the family home in Wellington. The painting was completed in Cleveland at the end of the following March in the studio of Willis Adams on Euclid Avenue near the Public Square. A plaque erected in 1932 marks this site.

Apparently Willard must have painted most of the canvas during the month of March. Young Devereux began posing after March 6, Willard's father died on March 14, and the painting was displayed in Ryder's studio March 27th. Devereux states it was completed by the 30th of March.

The Great Centennial Controversy

Both Western Reserve Historical Society in Cleveland, and Abbot Hall in Marblehead, have claimed to possess the **Centennial Canvas**. Of the two contenders, the **Spirit of '76** at Western Reserve appears much earlier than the painting now at Marblehead.

Over the years, identical photographs, supposedly of the **Centennial Painting**, have been issued by Willard, Ryder, and Marblehead. However, **neither** of these two paintings match the **Centennial Painting** photographs.

Cleveland Gray's Spirit of '76

To add to the confusion, there was a SECOND large **Spirit of '76** in existence shortly after the Centennial. On Valentine's Day in 1877, Willard presented an 8' x 13' **Spirit of '76** to the Cleveland Gray's Armory.

A large **Spirit of '76** was later destroyed there in the Armory fire of 1918. There are no known photographs identifying the Cleveland Gray's painting, as such, in existence today.

The Centennial Canvas Size

Needless to say, there are many conflicting theories on the **Centennial Spirit of '76**. The key to the mystery, however, seems to lie in the SIZE of the **Centennial Canvas** itself.

Unfortunately, the Art Catalogue at the Centennial does not list painting size. If it had, it would quickly solve the problem. However, in 1883, a short Willard biography, written by Willard's art associates in their monthly "Sketch Book," states:

"Mr. Willard produced his most ambitious work **Yankee Doodle**, a canvas 8' by 10' in size."

It is interesting to note that neither Barton, Ryder, nor Devereux mention the **Size** of the **Centennial Canvas** in any of their writings on Willard. It seems rather unusual in view of their numerous comments on the size of the other **Spirit of '76** paintings.

Willard seems to add to the conspiracy. In the 1912 "Cleveland Town Topics" interview, he refers to the **Centennial Painting** as a "Large Canvas." In the "Housekeeper" article of the same year, he is quoted as calling it a "Life Sized Canvas." However, in the "Everybody's Magazine" interview of 1917, whether intentional or not, Willard 'lets the cat out of the bag' —for he is quoted as saying the **Centennial Painting** was indeed "8' x 10' in size."

Ryder's Gift
(Western Reserve Historical Society)

Dr. Albert Benton, for many years associated with the Western Reserve Historical Society, attempted to establish their 4'4" x 6'10" **Spirit of '76** as the **Centennial Painting**. He contended that Willard could not have painted as large a canvas as 8' x 10' in the Willis Adams Studio, and that the 8' x 10' canvas was painted sometime later. His was a logical supposition in view of the primitive appearance of their painting, and its natural evolution from the lithograph of 1875. However, unknown to Dr. Benton, J. F. Ryder had explained the mystery of the **Western Reserve Spirit of '76** in letters he had written to Reverend Barton in 1895.

"I will send you in a day or two a photo from the (**Yankee Doodle**) Mr. Willard made for me for my new gallery . . . In the top story where will be my operating room (Garfield Building) is a series of openings between the beams forming a mansard roof.

"Those good fellows, the artists, are remembering the years when I was able to help them and are now giving me a handsome testimonial in painting something characteristic of their style to fill in those spaces or panels, 4½' wide and 7' long. Willard has already painted for me **Yankee Doodle** which will occupy a place of honor . .

"I think there is more fire, more energy of expression in this than in any former effort I fancy from my writing and our talking over, he has been newly enthused and given this painting more force. It is made for a decoration only, and less pains taken than in the former ones, but I feel it has a value in a sense beyond them.

"When you receive photo of new **Yankee Doodle** and note size and strength of

Ryder's Gift (SP-8) 1895
(W.R.H.S.)

H.M.L.

A photograph by Ryder plainly shows this painting, among others, displayed between the roof beams of his studio.

Photo of J. F. Ryder Studio.

Willard's name upon it, please understand I am accountable for it. It is my wish that all the pictures by my artistic friends be signed bold that all may know at once the artist."[23]

Marblehead Spirit of '76 (Devereux's Gift)

The **Marblehead Spirit of '76** is a magnificent canvas. It is the most often reproduced, and therefore the best known of all the paintings.

The main contender for the **Centennial Canvas** has generally been considered the **Marblehead Painting**. Willard and his associates all referred to the **Centennial Painting** as having gone on tour after 1876, and being purchased by General Devereux and presented to his home town of Marblehead, Mass., in 1880. A conflict arises, however, because there is no resemblance whatsoever, between the **Centennial Painting** photographs, and the painting now in Marblehead.

There is an additional problem in that it demonstrates an artistic expertise far too advanced for Willard's 1876 Centennial technique.

This discrepancy can be easily explained. The painting was returned to Willard in Cleveland in 1892, and for the sum of $500, Willard created a vastly improved **Spirit of '76**, repainting either the returned canvas, or possibly substituting a different canvas.

Spirit of '76

Available after January 1

Stamp collecting. For the fun of it.

Your Postal Service

Devereux's Purchases (SP-7) 1877/1892   (Abbot Hall, Marblehead, Mass.)

Photograph from Litchman's Photographers, Marblehead, Mass. Reportedly a photograph of the early Marblehead "Spirit of '76." It bears little resemblance to the painting in Marblehead today.

For a number of years, Marblehead would not even allow their painting to be photographed or reproduced. Devereux stated, "It was out of fear of damage to the original."[22] One wonders why Marblehead kept distributing photographs and lithographs of the **Centennial Painting**, even in recent years when the painting they owned looked considerably different.

Part of the problem can be attributed to the "town photographer," Litchman. I purchased several 8'' x 10'' photographs "of the **Marblehead Painting**" from their shop in the mid 1960's. They assured me that the photograph was taken in 1915. A close examination of the photograph indicates that it is the famous **Centennial Painting** photograph, and if this were indeed what the Marblehead Painting looked like in 1915, then it would be nearly impossible that Willard painted the Spirit of '76 that is in Marblehead today.

Fortunately, photographs of a **Spirit of '76**, extremely similar to Marblehead's current painting, first appeared in 1895, in Ryder's "The Painter of Yankee Doodle," "The New England Magazine." Therefore the painting did appear to exist shortly after the reported 1892 restoration, and most probably proceeded back to Marblehead. If Mr. Litchman's photograph was taken in 1915, it probably was a photocopy of an existing print, rather than a photo of the painting itself.

In the early 1970's, art experts from New York cleaned the **Marblehead Canvas**. With years of dirt and some paint removed, a few outlines of an earlier **Yankee Doodle** became apparent. Although far too little of the early **Yankee Doodle** is discernable to identify it as the **Centennial Painting,** there is definitely a signature on the broken cannon wheel that is NOT apparent in the **Centennial Photograph.**

It appears then that the **Marblehead Canvas** has been repainted, and in view of the quality of the painting, it was probably done during the 1892 restoration. The only question that remains is — did Willard restore the canvas returned to him, or did he overpaint another canvas? The only other **Spirit of '76** known to exist at that time was the **Cleveland Gray's** 8' x 13' painting completed in 1877.

In the 1930's Mrs. Henry K. Devereux stated to several persons, including Dr. Benton, that her father-in-law originally purchased the **Cleveland Gray's** painting—not the one that had been at the Centennial. Furthermore, he did not like the large cannon in the foreground, and returned the painting to Willard for restoration.

As a remote possibility, Willard could have reduced the height of the **Gray's** painting from 13' to 10' to remove the large cannon, and painted the canvas in its present form.

Only three years later, in 1895, Willard painted the **Western Reserve Spirit of '76** as a special gift for Ryder, and in attempting to recreate the original concept, included the large cannon in the foreground.

These theories are not all mine. Many have been suggested before. It has always been an either/or question between Western Reserve or Marblehead. It is a possibility that **The Centennial Spirit of '76** NO LONGER EXISTS. There is no reason to assume that any "unholy" agreement existed between Willard, his associates, and Marblehead. Willard painted "THE" Spirit of '76, he improved upon it, and it was sent to Marblehead. Willard wanted it remembered that way.

Is the **Centennial Painting** title all that important? Is one painting more significant than all the others? Are not all the paintings significant in their own right as Willard developed the evolution of the **Spirit of '76** story each successive time he sat before the canvas? These questions have unfortunately driven a wedge between Marblehead and Northern Ohio, when in reality these two areas should joyfully share a common heritage.

One question still remains. If the **Centennial Canvas** no longer exists—where has it gone?

If Willard sold Devereux the **Cleveland Gray's Painting**, perhaps the 8' x 10' **Centennial Spirit of '76** found a new home in the Cleveland Gray's Armory, and it was the **Centennial Painting**, then, that was burned in the Armory fire of 1918.

Another solution to the disappearance of the **Centennial Spirit of '76** is offered by Mr. Alden Hare, a onetime next door neighbor to the Willard family on Holyoke Ave. in Cleveland, and long time Willard buff. Mr. Hare has been quoted as saying that a large **Spirit of '76** was stored in the Willard basement after the turn of the century.

However, my favorite solution to the missing 1876 Canvas was offered by a Wellingtonian, who was somewhat disgusted with all the Centennial controversy. With tongue in cheek, he assured me that the missing **Centennial Canvas** was really the 2' x 3' **Spirit of '76** at Herrick Memorial Library in Wellington, shrunk from it's 8' x 10' size by improper laundering.

3. ADVANCED SKETCHES

"On to Havana"

A special sketch prepared for the Spanish American War appeared in the "Cleveland Plain Dealer" on May 15, 1898. Here the famous trio appear superimposed on an advancing contingent of Teddy Roosevelt's Rough Riders. The location of this work is unknown, but similar

On to Havana.

On to Havana (SP-15)   The Continental Soldier is now a "Rough Rider," the Fallen Soldier a Starving Cuban.

A.M.Willard

Cleveland Plain Dealer, May 15, 1898

sketches of the original trio are in existence.

4. LATER OILS

At least three oils appear to have been painted when Willard was in his late seventies. During this period, the artist's grandson, Willard Connally, replaced Devereux as the inspiration for the young drummer boy.

Thomas Gift

In 1912, Willard painted a 3' by 4' oil as a wedding present for his wife's nephew, John Thomas. Thomas prepared a special lithograph of this painting in 1926, and over the years acquired a sizeable collection of Willard's paintings. A prominent engineering consultant, Thomas was unfortunately institutionalized at the peak of his career, and was unable to fulfill a burning ambition to build a Willard museum in Wellington. Most of his collection was donated to the Herrick Memorial Library in Wellington in the late 1960s.

W.F.G.

Thomas Gift (SP-9) 1912   (Metromedia, Inc.)

The Thomas **Spirit of '76** was sold by Mrs. Agda Thomas to Captain L. L. Bucklew of Encinitas, California, in 1963. Bucklew and a group of fellow military veterans formed the San Diego Spirit of '76 Association to promote the patriotic theme of the painting. They distributed thousands of colored reproductions of the Thomas lithograph to school children throughout the nation.

With advancing years and limited finances, the painting was offered for sale and acquired by my family in 1968. For several years we attempted to carry on Bucklew's work, but soon sought someone with greater financial resources to properly publicize the painting and its message. The painting was subsequently purchased by Metromedia Inc., in 1972. It was reportedly on loan to the White House for a short time, and in 1975 enjoyed by millions of Americans as it began its journey as a featured exhibit on the Freedom Train.

W.F.G.

The author, his wife JoAnn, son Scott, and Capt. L. L. Bucklew with the Thomas Gift (SP-9) "Spirit of '76" in 1968.

Cleveland Commission—"The Original Masterpiece"

In 1912, the city of Cleveland commissioned Willard to paint them a large 8' by 10' **Spirit of '76**. The sum to be paid was reportedly $3,000.00. Local Cleveland Willard fans have entitled this canvas his "Original Masterpiece." It is more polished than the earlier paintings. Many agree, however, it does seem to lack the softness and charisma of the Marblehead painting. The artist's nephew, T. A. Willard, inventor and archaeologist, sums up this sentiment in a 1932 newspaper interview.

> "It is a fine painting from the standpoint of art, but there is not to me the same something that gives the thrill which comes to one who sees for the first time the old picture . . . he put something into his first picture—call it genius if you must—that is lacking in the one Cleveland owns."[24]

Devereux thought it was fitting that a replica be available in Cleveland where the **Spirit of '76** was "conceived and executed." He further stated:

> "This replica naturally is not as well executed as the original. This would be almost impossible at Willard's then advanced age (76). In this replica, Willard incorporated a number of changes. The coloring is different. He changed the arrangement of the stars from a circle of thirteen stars to a circle of nine, with four stars in the center. He

Cleveland Commission (SP-10) 1913   (Cleveland City Hall)

Barton's Gift (SP-11) 1916 (H.M.L.)

moderated the stride of the men. He changed the wounded soldier in the foreground to a more upright position."[25]

And last, but not least, Devereux mentioned what must have been his greatest concern,

"He changed the drummer boy . . . "

Barton Gift

Devereux only recognized the existence of three oils. He tells of one Willard painted for his friend, Rev. William Barton—in size 34" by 28".

"The painting was made in 1916 and really constitutes the third and last original painting of the **Spirit of '76** made by Mr. Willard. The original and the Cleveland replica are full size. This painting is really executed in miniature. Willard did not attempt to make an exact copy, hence, on this small painting there are many variations from the two larger paintings."[26]

Barton also donated this replica to the Herrick Memorial Library in Wellington.

5. WATER COLORS

In this later period of his life, Willard executed several small water colors, one 17½" by 23", signed but not dated; another 19" by 23", signed and dated 1916. Similar in appearance, both paintings at one time or another were in the possession of members of the Willard family, and eventually both found their way to the collection at the Western Reserve Historical Society.

W.F.G.

Water Color #1 (SP-12) 1916   (W.R.H.S.)

W.F.G.

Water Color #2 (SP-13) Circa 1916   (W.R.H.S.)

6. LITHOGRAPHS

It is important to recognize several significant lithographs, not only for their historical role in the **Spirit of '76** story, but to help in identifying them as lithographs in themselves, and not as separate paintings.

Centennial Chromo

The earliest of these is the chromolithograph prepared for the Centennial. In the lower right corner is the following inscription: "**Yankee Doodle**, 1776, Pub. by J. F. Ryder, Cleveland, Ohio." Although Ryder **may** have registered this lithograph with the Library of Congress, it is often confused with the Library of Congress Copyright #11242, which was issued for the

Original Design For a Painting sketch in 1875. The Centennial lithograph is important because it will help in identifying **The First Small Canvas** (the small oil prepared for the lithographers) and it also gives us a frame of reference for the original appearance of the large **Centennial painting.**

Babbits 1776 Soap Powder

The early commercial exploitations of **Yankee Doodle** were endless. One such example appeared as an advertisement in "Outlook" magazine. One could write to B. T. Babbitts 1776 Soap Powder in New York and receive a 24" by 18" colored panel of **Yankee Doodle**—pictures of an artist's proof and etching.

35

(Herrick Memorial Library)

Outlook Magazine

Willard at the age of 76 painting the Cleveland Commission "Spirit of '76."

Thomas Lithograph

It is important to stress the significance of the lithograph prepared by John Thomas in 1926, because of its frequent reproduction. Cleanings of the Thomas painting have eliminated several of the soldiers and muskets in the background, formerly prominent in the earlier lithograph.

Morgan Lithograph

In the late 1880's, Willard formed an association with the Morgan Lithographers in Cleveland. They, too, produced a number of his works by chromolithography. A new lithograph version of the **Spirit of '76**, 27″ by 36″, was prepared by Willard.

7. SIGNED AND HAND COLORED LITHOGRAPHS AND PHOTOS

Robert L. Walden, Wellington author, once put the count of "**Spirits of '76**" at 14. Unfortunately, he included a number of photographs and lithographs Willard handcolored and sometimes autographed in the last few years of his life. Several of these have reappeared in the northern Ohio area over the years. One autographed "to my daughter Maud" is in the possession of the General Tire and Rubber Co. in Akron. One executed for the Wellington Lodge F&AM, of which Willard was a member, appeared in the Wellington High School for a number of years and now is missing. This is probably the last work of his brush.

8. ASSOCIATED WORKS

Reverend Samuel Willard

In his early years, Willard painted several family portraits. Two such portraits of Willard's father, Reverend Samuel Willard are known to exist today. He also displayed a small sculpture of the "old drummer" in Cleveland in the early 1900's. It's location is unknown.

Hugh Mosher

Willard's favorite subject was Hugh Mosher. There are references to several sketches—a photograph of one is at Herrick Memorial Library. A large 2/3 life size oil of the fifer, 24″ x 46″, is also at Herrick Memorial Library.

Detail Studies

Willard evidently executed a large number of small **Spirit of '76** detail studies in water color. Many of these were reportedly loaned to "one of the Cleveland newspapers" in the 1920's or 1930's. Two remained in the Willard family and are the only ones accountable for today. Both measure 8½″ by 7″. One is a detailed study of the old drummer's right hand, the other his left hand. They, along with several other Willard paintings, were donated to Western Reserve Historical Society by Willard's great-nephew, Alfred R. Willard of Cleveland.

Hugh Mosher, The Fifer (P-33)
Circa 1890   (H.M.L.)

Diamond Shamrock Corp.

possibly be one of the water color replicas owned by the Willard family.

St. Paul
In a newspaper clip, Waldon Fawcett tells us **"Yankee Doodle** was only 24″ x 28″ in size and was purchased by a gentleman in St. Paul."[27]

Wellington High School
Were there **two Spirit of '76** paintings that for years hung in the dark corridors of the Wellington High School? One has definitely been identified as a colored photograph; however, John J. Thomas, Jr., in an address in 1932 stated:

> "The replica in the Wellington High School assembly room, Uncle Arch told me, was the last copy of the **Spirit of '76** he executed."[28]

Burned Spirits
In an April 1919 article in "The Ladies Home

W.F.G.

Old Drummer Left Hand (SP-102)   (W.R.H.S.)

W.F.G.

Old Drummer Right Hand (SP-101)   (W.R.H.S.)

Wood Sculpture
As late as 1936, a wood sculpture by Willard of the **Spirit of '76** belonged to the Willard estate. Its present location is unknown.

9. FACT OR FICTION?

Senile Jabez
Another interesting tale comes from a Challacombe descendent related to Willard through his sister-in-law, Rebecca Challacombe. It seems Rebecca's husband, Jabez, in a state of senility, became so attached to their personal family replica of the **Spirit of '76** that he cut it from the frame, rolled it into a pillow, never to leave his sight or touch. Needless to say, the painting was discarded after the old man's death.

Willard Battery Co.
Reportedly another oil adorned the walls of the main office of the Willard Battery Co. in Cleveland. This painting, however, might

Journal," Reverend William Barton refers to "three or four **smaller** copies of the picture, **two of these were burned.**" The only record of a burned **Spirit of '76** was the **LARGE** painting destroyed by the fire in the Cleveland Gray's Armory the previous year in 1918.

WHICH ORIGINAL?
Which then was the "original?" The original what? The original cartoon? The original sketch? The original design for a painting? The original canvas? The original Centennial painting? The original masterpiece? If I must pick an "original" favorite, and I have seen and studied them all, then it must be that heroic canvas at Marblehead. For I, too, like Devereux and thousands of other Americans, have stood in reverence and awe and there "swallowed a lump that will sometimes come in one's throat."[17]

And how many **Spirits of '76** did he create? Only time will tell.

CHAPTER III

The Artist and His Works

THE EARLY YEARS—1836-1853

Archibald McNeal Willard was born in Bedford, Ohio, on August 22, 1836, the fourth of seven children in the family of Reverend Samuel R. and Catherine Willard. His grandfather, Jonathan Willard, also residing with the family, was a veteran of the Revolutionary War, having fought as a member of the Vermont Green Mountain Boys, and was present at the surrender of General Burgoyne. The old soldier was a close and constant companion to the young boy. His many tales of battle were later to influence the artist's conception of **The Spirit of '76.**

Reverend Samuel R. Willard, a fundamentalist preacher, moved his family frequently from parish to parish throughout the northern Ohio, Western Reserve area. There was little money for more than the basic necessities of life.

Of this heritage, Willard wrote,

> "My father was not only a deeply religious man, but a man of strong patriotic spirit. He inherited from his father, and I from him, an ardent love of country and pride in its glory."[29]

The Artist's Parents

W.F.G.

Rev. Samuel R. Willard (P-12) Circa 1870
(Willard F. Gordon Col.)

Bedford Historical Society

Etching by Roy Hern. Willard's birthplace, Bedford, Ohio. This home is still in use.

Willard tells of his early education and his first plunge into art.

> "My father . . . was able only to give me a common school education. I made better use of my educational opportunities than I

W.F.G.

Catherine Willard (P-13) Circa 1870
(Willard F. Gordon Col.)

Early Humorous Sketch, Circa 1850's (H.M.L.) This was later developed into a lithograph "My Grandfather's Clock" published by J. F. Ryder. (A-77)

H.M.L.

sometimes seemed to be doing, for I learned readily and remembered what I learned."[30] . . . "Like all boys, I was not anxious to ruin my health by too much school work'[31] . . . "I often seemed to be idle when I was drawing pictures on my slate; while caricatures of the teacher and cartoons of incidents in school life sometimes got me into trouble."[32]

"I made frequent use of my slate and pencil—actually discovering after a time that I could draw a house that showed both front and sides; could even create a cow that did not need horns to distinguish it from a horse."[33]

Later in life his friends were to write:

"From his earliest boyhood picture making was a passion with him. At school the mathematical problems disappeared from his slate in a maze of houses, dogs, cows, and all manner of pictures. The primitive conditions surrounding him made it necessary for him to devise the material wherewith to exercise his skill. This he was equal to, and he himself relates with much gusto his first effort on a large scale, when during the

sugaring season, he stripped the outer bark from the large beech trees within the sugar camp and with red chalk and charred embers from the camp fire he produced upon the trees painted savages of fierce and hideous mien, greatly to the admiration of the elders, and the terror of the youngsters. The trees in the vicinity were made to receive the impress of the boy artist's jackknife, and remnants of his carvings still remain."[34]

It is said his budding talents became evident on many a board fence, barn, and outhouse door as the following tale will attest.

"One morning in the gray of an early summer dawn, he was called from his bed to see a page from the Arabian Nights moving slowly down the hilly roads . . . Welch Delevan's Circus flitting by night from Chagrin Falls exhibit of Tuesday to that of a neighboring town on Wednesday.

"The Reverend Willard . . . had recently completed a frame barn, the wide front door of which was still untouched of paint. The departing carpenters had left behind them fragments of red chalk and charcoal . . .

40

Blown to a white heat of artistic enthusiasm by the delirium of color and motion the long procession had thrust upon him, the boy could hardly wait until breakfast was over and his father started to the village to unearth the cache of charcoal and chalk he made under the horsemanger. Mounted on an upturned box, he began on the virgin wood of the barn door. Camels, elephants, piebald steeds; musicians asleep on the gilded chariot; tired and road-weary women in wagons; troops of ponies moving listlessly along; the wagons, the cages; moved in procession of red and black across the door.

"When the father rode into the yard, with the westering sun at his back and the scared boy watching him from the leafy covert of a maple tree, his first thought was of a birch gad, but he sensed better of it, and sent the boy to a fellow-minister who had dabbled in local portrait-painting, where he remained for several weeks; the beginning and the ending of his boyhood education in art. 'As for the barn door,' said Mr. Willard, 'it was for some days the wonder of the neighborhood.'"[35]

One tale passed down through the Willard family tells of a painting on the back of Reverend Samuel Willard's backyard outhouse. Unfortunately, the drawing was a remarkably good likeness of the old parson himself seated within the outhouse, complete with trousers around his ankles. It was several days before Reverend Willard's attention was drawn to the rear of his outhouse where he then first viewed the work of art that had become the talk of the neighborhood. It took little time or effort to determine who was the offending artist. Young Archibald did not escape a good thrashing with the birch gad this time.

EARLY WELLINGTON - 1853-1863

The Willards settled permanently in Wellington in 1855 where Reverend Samuel Willard ministered to the local Disciples of Christ Church. Several years earlier, Archibald apprenticed himself to E. S. Tripp, a decorative artist, wheelwright and wagon maker. Willard proved a valuable asset, and quickly outstripped his master in ability. Of these years he writes:

"Little cities like Wellington had their carriage factories, and the makers vied with those of neighboring towns, and strove for excellence of craftsmanship and beauty of ornamentation.

"Mr. Tripp always had a display of his wagons and carriages at the county fair. The vehicles built for these exhibits were finished with special care, and farmers were pleased to drive a wagon or buggy that had taken a blue ribbon. I began painting little vignettes on the sides of these exhibit

H.M.L.

Village of Wellington (A-93) 1857   (H.M.L.)
One of Willard's earliest oils. Several of these stately old houses still stand in the picturesque Village of Wellington.

wagons, and dainty designs on carriages and buggies . . ."[36]

"I let my imagination have free reign in executing landscapes, ships, medallions of Washington and Ben Franklin and others."[37]

"These ornaments, added to honest workmanship in wood and iron, gave Mr. Tripp's carriages a deserved reputation, and kept alive in me the actual use of brush in other than strictly commercial pursuits. Now and then I would pick up a bit of leather or oilcloth from an old carriage cover and paint a picture upon it. These paintings hung about the shop, and as some of them were admired and asked for, I gave them away."[38]

H.M.L.

Tripp Carriage Factory   (H.M.L.)
Willard is standing on second floor porch.

41

Willard in Band Uniform with horn. (H.M.L.)

and as such, it must be regarded as a brilliant achievement, the likeness is most striking—almost faultless."[39]

Willard's artistic talents appeared everywhere in Wellington. He provided a special surprise for the Foote family when their new sleigh was delivered, personally embellished with a portrait of their favorite coach dog.

A Mr. A. G. Couch won first prize at the 1857 Wellington Agricultural Fair for his furniture—hand-painted and decorated by young Archibald Willard.

Primitive portraits of young Wellington children filled the artist's canvas, often humorously recording an impish or unpleasant expression in the young face. Pastoral landscapes of creek, hill, and forest found their way into many local homes. Many of the landscapes were adequately adorned with cows and sheep, for Wellington had become the leading milk and cheese center for northern Ohio.

The tall, 6′ 3″ lanky boy who acquired the nickname "Deke" or "Deacon," was a familiar figure in Wellington. Along with his brother Charles, Archibald was a member of the Wellington Silver Cornet Band.

In 1860, James A. Garfield, later to become the 20th president of the United States, preached the dedication sermon at Rev. Samuel R. Willard's new church. Garfield was an old family friend. Later in the 1880's, Archibald completed both a portrait and sculpture of Garfield. Their presence is unknown, but of the sculpture Willard's art associates wrote:

"Mr. Willard's versatility is most strikingly shown in the production quite recently of bust of President Garfield. This is Mr. Willard's first effort with the modeler's clay,

Landscape painted on top of commode.

Furniture from the A. G. Couch Co. Hand painted by Willard.

W.F.G.

H.M.L.

Eniolus Willard (P-4) Circa 1860 (Geauga Co. Historical Society)

Hattie Adel Pratt (Blue Girl) (P-9) Circa 1865 (Herrick Memorial Library)

Both these young children were painted from photographs after their deaths.

W.F.G.

W.F.G.

Emma Bennett (P-6) Circa 1870 (Edward S. Wells Col.) Willard humorously recorded her scornful distaste for posing.

Tripp Girls (P-5) Circa 1865 (Herrick Memorial Library) Daughters of Willard's employer, E. S. Tripp.

The Artist at work.   H.M.L.
                                                       (H.M.L.)

One of Willard's first commissioned works was a large mysterious canvas of pre-historic dinosaurs prepared for a traveling lecturer who ordered it to illustrate a lecture he was scheduled to give on the "Marvels of the Natural World." Unfortunately, the lecturer was enticed into joining a local card game, unaware that a few of the Wellington boys were quite proficient in "indoor sports." Unable to produce the agreed upon price of $25.00, the lecturer left town a little wiser, but without the painting. A local merchant, William Vischer, not wishing to see Willard cheated out of his commission, produced the money and became the new owner of the painting.[40] Unfortunately, this painting too has disappeared.

A master of graffiti, sketches and caricatures appeared most any place Willard might have a few idle moments to spend with pencil in hand. The walls of the Tripp factory attested to his humor. The closets and attic of his family home were equally adorned. Cartoon sketches of the faces of local men, attributed to the Willard Brothers, hung on the walls of "Herrick's Hornet's Nest," a local general store which was complete with pot belly stove, hard back chairs, and a sawdust box "within spitting distance."

The Hornet's Nest was a man's store, the neighborhood forum, a meeting place on those cold or rainy days when there was no man's work to be done.[41] Discussions were lively—the most prevalent subject was that of slavery. Wellington was especially sensitive to the issue. The town served as one of the final stops on the

"Underground Railway." For the runaway slave, there remained only a few miles to Lake Erie, then on to Canada and freedom.

The social and religious, as well as political issues of slavery, which in time would lead to war, weighed heavily on the mind of the young artist.

THE WAR YEARS—1863-1865

Willard enlisted as color sergeant in the 86th Ohio Volunteer Infantry soon after the outbreak of the Civil War. He served with this unit seeing action in Kentucky and Tennessee. Throughout this period his pencil was not idle.

"During the Civil War, I was a soldier, and I drew pictures of camp and army life and sent them in letters to my friends. Other soldiers saw and wanted them, and some of my sketches were photographed and sold. I still have some pictures which I made while our regiment lay at Cumberland Gap. These pictures while crude enough in some of their aspects, have a simple fidelity which made them popular among the soldiers, and enabled them to supplement their home letters with some pictorial representations. The simplicity with which these sketches told their main story made the soldiers charitable toward their artistic imperfections. They helped the folks at home to understand a little better some of the conditions of our army life.

". . . I had another strong quality which entered into whatever work I did and that was a love of fun. Even the grim pictures of battlefields had in them little elements of humor which, incongruously enough, found their way into my memories. These brighten-

                                                       W.F.G.
The Awkward Squad (A-3) Circa 1863-1865   (W.R.H.S.)
Sergeant addressing two new awkward recruits.

Battle of Cumberland Gap (CW-1) Circa 1863   (H.M.L.)
J. F. Ryder photographed and sold reproductions of Willard's Civil War sketches. The original sketches have disappeared. This is the lower right quarter of one of the photo reproductions.

ed the horrors of war, and for the ability to perceive the humor of a hard situation, I have always been thankful.''[42]

Many Wellington area boys served in the Ohio Volunteers. Hugh Mosher and his fife would be immortalized by the artist some twelve years later. Unlike Mosher, Willard escaped unscathed from the battles of war, but had a near fatal bout with dysentery, saved only by the personal attention of his closest friend, Harry Bennett.

In February, 1864, Willard's unit was mustered out of the service and he returned to Wellington. At this time, Willard made his first contact with J. F. Ryder, the latter photographing and printing several of Willard's Civil War sketches. Willard's sketches also are reported to have been printed in Harper's Magazine.

This same year he married his Wellington sweetheart, Nellie S. Challacombe. No reason is given why the young artist left his new bride to return to the war, but less than a year later, in February 1865, Willard re-enlisted in 176 Ohio Volunteers as a private. He saw action in Nashville, being discharged there several months later in June of 1865.

Again Willard returned to his home in Wellington. Of this he writes:

"When the war was over I had a great ambition. It was to make a great panorama of war scenes and exhibit them all over the country. Such things were not common then . . . I undertook to tell the story of the war in pictures six feet tall and twelve feet long, sewed end to end, . . . and rolled in two rollers, so that the painting could be rolled on in succession, and explained in a lecture.

"While doing this work, I learned several things I had not previously known about drawing. At first the shadows in my pictures all fell back from the objects, as if cast by seven different suns, and my flags were blown back by five or six different winds. But before the canvas was ready for exhibition, I had corrected some of the more glaring faults, and I was sure that I had embarked on a career of an artist, and one that would bring me fame and fortune.

"I still smile as I recall those too-confident hopes and sigh when I remember how they were dashed to earth. The panorama was not a financial success. People had seen too much of the war and wanted to forget it. We gave a very few exhibitions to diminishing audiences, and then packed our panorama away in the loft of a barn.

"It was a great grief to me to have wasted so much good cotton cloth, and time and

45

paint, as well as hope and patriotic ardor. They were all lost except the cloth. The paints were of a quality that could be washed out and we washed them out to save the cloth for domestic purposes.

"Thus my first artistic ambition went to suds, and I set myself to the commonplace task of earning a living."[43]

THE EMERGING ARTIST—1865-1875

Willard returned to his work at the Tripp factory where his brothers, Robert, Samuel and Charles, also endowed with an artistic flair, were employed at the carriage shop.

"Willard used a novel way to collect a bad debt. He had painted a beautiful basket of fruit on the sleigh of a farmer. Payment was not made for some time. Mr. Willard saw his chance one day when the farmer and sleigh were in town. Grabbing his paints, he drew a big black worm crawling out of a luscious apple. Needless to say, the farmer came the next day to pay off the bad debt plus an extra charge to have the worm painted out."[44]

Archibald and Nellie lived with his parents for a number of years. The family soon swelled in size with the addition of the artist's first three children—Charles, born in 1865, Maud in 1868, and Harry in 1869.

Life settled into a peaceful routine. There were more Wellington portraits to paint. Often a grieving parent would present the artist with a tintype photo of a recently deceased child. Willard would then prepare a life size oil or

W.F.G.

Everett Morton Gott (P-19) Circa 1885 (Willard F. Gordon Col.) Everett, a distant nephew of Willard, died at the age of five. The artist's only known existing Chalk Pastel, portrays a sweet but pallid countenance. In the lower left foreground is a toy cart and doll—in the background, fence and cottage—familiar objects in Willard's paintings.

pastel of the child, embellished with an extravagant landscape background. Often he realistically included the last remembered sickly pallor in coloring the child's skin.

PREPARE TO PUCKER.

(H.M.L.)

46

OUR FIRST PARENTS —BEFORE THE FALL,

AND AFTER.

(H.M.L.)

THE GIDDY PLUMBER.

All the forenoon he "soft soldered" the Cook,
Then seventeen dollars he charged in his book.

Contentment is Better than Riches.

47

Pluck I and Pluck II Lithographs registered by Ryder with the Library of Congress in 1872.

During this period, there were more local landscapes and always the humorous sketches and caricatures. Willard liked to parody expressions and sayings of the times with cartoon sketches. Some of the better known are:

> "Contentment is better than riches."
> "An ounce of prevention is worth a pound of cure."
> "A stitch in time saves nine."
> "Many a slip twixt cup and lip."

PLUCK

One day, Tripp's daughter, Addie, brought Willard a crude woodcut from a children's paper called "The Nursery." It showed a dog harnessed to a wagon, chasing a rabbit. She requested him to make an enlarged copy for her.

The idea appealed to the artist's sense of humor, and he set to work with great zeal, creating a new version of this theme. This humorous work, entitled "Pluck," proved to be the turning point in Willard's artistic career. For models, he used his three children and the family dog.

The painting was sent to J. F. Ryder in Cleveland for framing. Ryder questioned Willard as to the outcome of the race—the result was Willard's creation of "Pluck II." Both paintings were placed on display in Ryder's window. Ryder comments:

> "No one could look upon that race unmoved and the spirit of fun appealed to all. The men who had driven a similar vehicle as boys enjoyed it heartily."

A friend of Ryder's from the "Cleveland Plain Dealer" wrote him the following note:

> "I want you to take those pictures out of your window; they are making my life a misery . . . the fun in those pictures makes me laugh . . . I've got a crack in my lip and I break it open afresh every day."
>
> Ryder continues:
> "A score of people came in each day to inquire if they were paintings or chromos, and what was their price. Many wanted to know if I was not going to have chromos, and to put their names down for a pair then and there. I became convinced that if I did not have chromos made of the pictures, it would be a mistake."[45]

Ryder secured copyrights under the title of **Pluck #1** and **Pluck #2** and went to New York to find a publisher. He was repeatedly advised to abandon this undertaking as the only marketable chromos were "illuminated mottos representing scriptural subjects and texts."[46] Ryder proved them all wrong. His first printing of 2,000 pair was an immediate sellout, and all told, some 10,-000 sets were rolled off the stone at $10.00 per pair. Willard stated:

> "The royalties from the sale of these photographs added to my income and increased my determination to be an artist. I studied art with such consistency as I could, while continuing my work in the carriage shop."[47]

Over the years, Willard created numerous replicas of the **Pluck** Series, sometimes using a rabbit, sometimes a cat as the object of the chase. But there was always the same story—the dog with wagon attached, in hot pursuit, determination and fear in the children's faces, and their final disasterous impact with a fallen log.

DEACON JONES' EXPERIENCE

Ryder tells us of Willard's second successful chromo.

> "The phenomenal success of the publication of **Pluck** naturally led to other pictures. The artist had, as a story teller with a brush, felt the pulse of the public. He found the public liked to laugh, and was encouraged to go farther in the same direction. One day he brought in to me a painting representing, in a room in a farmhouse which was evidently at once kitchen, dining-room and parlor, a family upon their knees at prayer, the supplicant, the father of the family with a cat upon his back and the mischievous boys setting the small dog upon the cat. It was the most laughable situation possible; but I felt that it would not do to publish the picture. I feared that one might see a possible sacrilegious tinge that might prove disastrous to its success. After hesitating over it for several days, it occurred to me that Bret Harte, who had in many ways shown his ability to skim over the thin ice of public opinion in matters of religious sentiment, might prove a valuable ally. So with a letter in my pocket to Mr. Harte, . . . I started for New York, . . . to pave the way to Mr. Harte's launching the picture safely upon the public.
>
> "I found the famous author, delivered my letter and showed him a photograph of the painting which amused him greatly. I told him I wanted that picture made the subject of a poem in his peculiar vein. He said he would try it. The business details were arranged to our mutual satisfaction, and he agreed to meet me three days later at a certain bookstore on Broadway, which he made headquarters when in the city. He came at the appointed time with his poem and read it to me bubbling over with laughter as he read. He had named the poem **Deacon Jones' Experience**, and, of course, that named the picture."[48]

The price agreed upon was only $250, just half the usual rate, the poem to be released as a joint venture, Hart to add it to a new book of published works, Ryder to release its publication as a prelude to the chromo sales. Unfortunately, Hart

Deacon Jones' Experience, Circa 1873 (H.M.L.)

was ready to publish before Ryder. A dispute followed. Hart then wrote:

"Buy me out. Send me your check for $200, publish the thing yourself just when and where it will best suit you. . . . Remember I should have asked $500 for the thing, out and out, for I feel I should have all the parsons after me."

(signed) Bret Harte[49]

Deacon Jones' Experience

"Ye're right when you lays it down, Parson,
    Thet the flesh is weak and a snare;
And to keep yer plow in the furrow—
    When yer cattle begins to rare—
Ain't no sure thing. And, between us,
    The same may be said of prayer.

Why I stood the jokes, on the river,
    Of the boys, when the critters found
Thet I'd jined the church, and the snicker
    Thet, maybe ye mind, went 'round,
The day I set down with the mourners,
    In the old camp-meetin' ground!

I stood all that, and I reckon
    I might at a pinch stood more—
For the boys, they represents Bael,
    And I stands as the Rock of the Law;
And it seemed like a moral scrimmage,
    In holdin' agin their jaw.

But thar's crosses a Christian suffers,
    As hezn't got that pretense—
Things with no moral purpose,
    Things ez hez got no sense;
Things ez, somehow, no profit
    Will cover their expense.

Yes, I think, with the Lud's assistance,
    I might have continered then,
If, gettin' her holt, that kitten
    Hedn't dropped her claw in me—when
It somehow reached the 'Old Adam,'
    And I jumped to my feet with 'Amen.'

So, ye're right when you say it, Parson,
    Thet the flesh is weak and a snare;
And to keep yer plow in the furrow—
    When yer cattle begins to rare—
Ain't no sure thing. And, between us,
    I say it's just so with prayer.

Ez how! I was jest last evenin'
    Addressin' the Throne of Grace,
And mother knelt in the corner,
    And each of the boys in his place—
When that sneakin' pup of Keziah's
    To Jonathan's cat giv chase!

I never let on to mind 'em.
    I never let on to hear;
But driv that prayer down the furrow
    With the cat hidin' under my cheer,
And Keziah a-whisperin', 'Sic her!'
    And mother a-sayin', 'You dare!'

I asked fer a light fer the heathen,
    To guide, on his narrow track,
With that dog and that cat jest waltzin',
    And Jonathan's face jest black,
When the pup made a rush and the kitten—
    Dropped down on the small of my back."[50]

Copyright and Published by   J. F. RYDER, Cleveland, O.
IN THIS WHEAT BYE AND BYE.

(H.M.L.)

Willard accompanied Ryder to New York in 1873 and remained there several weeks to study art under J. O. Eaton. It was his only formal art training. The artist greatly profited from the experience, for in only two years his **Roman Prisoner** was acclaimed by the Academy of Design in New York. It was subsequently sold with an additional painting, **Venus,** to a Cleveland dentist, Dr. F. M. Clark—the pair commanding the handsome sum of $1,500.

Holidays were always special times for most of the folks in Wellington. One favorite occasion was the Fourth of July celebration. The ever popular martial music band, led by Hugh Mosher's fife, highlighted the day. Willard stated:

"He could play the fife better than any man I ever knew of."[51]

Mosher's favorite drummer was Freeman Greene, who was irreverently nicknamed "Three Finger Dick." An earlier hand injury had dis-

H.M.L.

Roman Prisoner (A-11) Circa 1874   (H.M.L.)

qualified Greene from service in the Civil War. Despite the handicap, according to Ryder, Greene could

> "vary the roll by beating intervals upon the chime of his drum instead of the head. He was in the habit also of throwing his sticks into the air to perform a succession of somersaults and be caught on the way down and driven into the roll again without missing a note as if nothing happened."[52]

Freeman Greene was indirectly identified with Mosher in Willard's original **Yankee Doodle** cartoon. In fact, the drummer even posed for a few photographs at Sawtelles. Unfortunately for Greene, fate chose not to bring him fame.

Willard traveled frequently to Cleveland working with Ryder in the production of the humorous **Pluck** and **Deacon Jones** chromolithographs. One day Ryder said to Willard, "Why don't you work up something for the Centennial?" "I'll think about it," replied Willard.

THE MATURING ARTIST—1876-1895

1875 and 1876 were **Yankee Doodle** years. There was time for little else. The work was begun in Wellington. Sketches were drawn, discarded, and redrawn. Photographs were taken and retaken—long, still poses before the camera of William Sawtelle. An idea was born, but it was far from fruition.

By the winter of 1875—1876, Willard had transferred his easel to Cleveland. Here was the large well-lighted studio of Willis Adams, the more advanced camera and technique of J. F. Ryder, and less distraction of family and dogs. Freeman Greene could not take the time from his business obligations to travel to Cleveland to pose as the old drummer. Willard sent for his father to replace him.

At last it was finished. The Cleveland newspapers had immediate praise:

> "A thrilling picture and a worthy contribution to the cause of patriotism."[53]

With the Centennial in Philadelphia came national and international recognition and fame.

> "Willard is a rising star in the art world of America."
> "Should Willard enter deeper into the spirit of historic painting, he will doubtless be the first genuine national painter of America."[54]

The whole Willard family soon moved to Cleveland and shared in the limelight. The family again increased in size—a son, Albert, was born in 1877, but, unfortunately, died the same

ARCHIBALD M. WILLARD
at the age of forty, when he painted the "Spirit of '76"

H. K. Devereux
"The Spirit of '76"

Six months later, the "Cleveland Herald" was a little more patronizing—

> "A moment's thought will show . . . a thousand and one reasons why an Academy should be sustained."[56]

By the 1880's, the Academy was incorporated to "establish and maintain a gallery of art, to collect works of art, and to provide for their sale and proper preservation."[57]

Willard was a principal director and teacher. He was listed as instructing in "Portraiture and landscape; classes in oil or black and white; and sketch and life classes drawing from the undraped figure."[58] The fee for the season was $5.00.

The Academy held frequent exhibitions. Willard's latest works were featured prominently, and were often highly acclaimed.

The Academy published a monthly magazine, "The Sketch Book," "It is simply, as its name fully implies, a volume of sketches—a book of choice quotations from the artist's portfolio, as it were" . .[59] Many of Willard's sketches were reproduced "on the stone" for the "Sketch Book"—several landscapes, old mills and locks, not to mention cows and sheep, a caricature of the Academy's members during an outing at Lake Chautauqua, a lovely young girl in **Grandma's Chair,** and an impish boy on a stool.

One issue included a Willard biography. His friends wrote quite highly of him—

> "He owes his success as an artist to his own untiring industry aided by an original versatility, somewhat remarkable. A strong physical organization embodied in over six feet of perpendicular bone and muscle, a marked individuality and a quaint irresistable humor renders him a most genial and companionable friend . . . Archie, or "The Deacon," is a most engaging host to his many friends."[60]

WELLINGTON MURALS

William Rininger, an old Wellington friend, employed Willard to paint two handsome murals on the east and west walls of his vestibule—one of a soldier in full armor and spear, and the other of "Nydia" the Pompeiian flower firl. For many years, these walls were papered over, rediscovered in 1910 and rescued, lath, plaster and all, when the building was torn down in the 1950's.

year. Son Byron was born in 1879, and a daughter, Catherine, in 1881.

Willard was prominent in the development and encouragement of art in the Cleveland area. He was an original member of the "Old Bohemians," an informal gathering of artists, mostly of German stock. By 1877, the group developed into the Cleveland Art Club, and they, in turn, renamed the organization the Academy of Art. For awhile, the Academy rented rooms in the Cleveland City Hall. It seems the city was not quite ready for such a large dose of culture. "The Cleveland Herald" reports:

> "Question of leasing rooms in the City Hall to the Academy of Fine Arts . . . opposed on the grounds the rent asked was too little and result would be a tax upon the general public, who are in no way interested in fine arts."[55]

M-4

M-5

The Wellington Murals

(S.L.C.H.S.)

THE LOCK • A·M·Williard

A-84 (Cleveland Public Library)

Sketchbook, 1883

54

+·THE·OLD·SHAKER MILL·+·A·M·Williard·+

A-82 (Cleveland Public Library)

Sketchbook, 1883

A.M.W.

STUDY OF COW & SHEEP A.M. WILLIARD.

A-83 (Cleveland Public Library)

Sketchbook, 1883

The Spirit of Electricity   (Washington Court House, Ohio)

WASHINGTON COURT HOUSE MURALS

Max Cook, Cleveland decorator and painting contractor was a good friend of Arch Willard. Max thought Willard was a genius, and employed the artist to paint frescos and stucco reliefs in many northern Ohio churches, homes of prominent citizens, and public buildings. Willard decorated most of the New Cleveland Opera House in the early 1880's. In 1882, Max accepted a bid for $2,445 for fresco work on the county court house in Washington Court House, Ohio. Many years later, Mrs. Cook, then a widow, stopped by the court house to see "The Willard Murals." Surprised court house officials had not paid too much attention to the three classic murals—each a heroic size female with flowing robes—Three Spirits: **The Spirit of Electricity,** the **Spirit of U.S. Mail,** and the **Spirit of the Telegraph.** The murals were given close inspection. In the hand of one young lady, the **Spirit of U.S. Mail,** was an envelope on which the artist had lettered part of his name—"A.M. Will—Cleveland, Ohio." Other Washington Court

The Spirit of the U.S. Mail

Diamond Shamrock Corp.

(Miss M. Moore)

The Spirit of the Telegraph

Fayette Co. Historical Society

House officials mentioned mysterious art on the back of filing cabinets—it proved to be Willard graffiti.

The living room of a local home, the temporary residence of the visiting artist, was elaborately decorated with floral vignettes, reminiscent of the Tripp wagon days. Washington Court House will long remember that Arch Willard came to town.

Jim Bludso

In 1878, Willard painted a picture of Jim Bludso, a riverboat captain immortalized in a poem by Col. John Hay, Secretary of State under McKinley. Bludso manned the wheel of his burning ship—"I'll hold her nozzle agin the bank 'till the last Galoot's ashore."

A reporter for the "Cleveland Herald" wrote the following account of this painting and its reception at the Cleveland Exhibition.

"Jim Bludso's heroic effort, as told so vividly by the poet, has added reality after one has gazed on Willard's last effort. The determined face, with the eyes that fairly blaze with excitement and yet bespeak firm resolution, the disheveled hair, the tense muscles of the arm, the death grip of the hand on the pilot wheel, which means life to all on board but Bludso, the lurid glaze from the flames of the doomed steamer are strongly wrought by the artist who seems to have bent all his energies and talents to the task. The painting, and notably the face, will repay close study, but it is to be hoped it will have very few such unappreciative observers as the couple that stopped before it last night. Said she, "Look here, will you. There's a picture of a maniac, ain't it?"[61]

Willard must have cringed at that reaction. He personally had modeled for the face of Jim Bludso, capturing his image reflected in a mirror illuminated by a flickering kerosene lantern.

W.F.G.

Allegorical Birth of the Flag (A-9) Circa 1877   (W.R.H.S.)
Christopher Columbus, Martin Luther, and George
Washington—receiving the inspiration for the design of the
American Flag.

A.M.Willard

H.M.L.

Jim Bludso (A-51) Circa 1878
Willard self-portrait — modeled by lantern light.

Certainly one of Willard's most unusual paintings was the allegorical **Divine Origin of the
American Flag.** With his fame as the painter of
the patriotic **Yankee Doodle,** it is only natural
that he was sought out to portray the inspirations
of other patriots.

Mr. Charles Latimer, a business associate of
General Devereux, was president of the Anti-
Metric Society. It was his contention that if God
wanted the United States on the Metric System,
he certainly would have revealed his plan to the
American forefathers—

> "Mr. Latimer proposed the ideal group of
> figures to include Martin Luther,
> Christopher Columbus, and George Wash-
> ington, each one emblematic of a great
> step forward in the March of Civilization

toward personal freedom as now is established in America. The origin of the National
Flag was represented by alternate bars of
blue and glowing red, as seen in the sky at
dawn by the reflection of the first light of
day upon the wave lines of summer clouds
with the stars of early morning intermingled
against the blue background."[62]

The August 26, 1878 "Cleveland Herald" kindly
said, "It will be more of interest to the student of
history, than to the ordinary observer."[63] The
large 10′ by 12′ canvas was lost for a number of
years, but reappeared in 1901 at a warehouse
auction sale. It was bid upon to serve as a waterproof cover "for some goods that might be ex-
posed to the weather."[64] The painting found its
way back into the limelight, was stored in the
basement of the Cleveland Museum of Art in the
1930's, and they subsequently, most graciously,
'unloaded' it on the Western Reserve Historical
Society.

Willard's talents were not idle where local
issues were concerned. His political cartoons
appeared in numerous northern Ohio newspapers.

No task was too small or too great for his pen.
Willard headed an artistic committee to design
an emblem for the City of Cleveland, and drew
the pictures for his friend, Rev. Barton's
children's book, "The Story of a Pumpkin Pie."

* * * * * * * *

Book Illustrations (A-44)
Another version of the "Pluck" theme.
"The Story of a Pumpkin Pie"
Verse by William E. Barton

58

"They harnessed Towser to the cart
And for the garden lot did start.
The pumpkin loaded they with skill,
While Helen held old Towser still."

"O Doctor Watts, thou didst not right
In telling dogs to bark and bite!
O Towser, thou didst little know
How great the wreck thy wrath would show!"

Minute Men of the Revolution (A-15)   (The Union Club, Cleveland)

One of his finest patriotic paintings, **Minute Men of the Revolution,** depicts a Revolutionary War family—the husband and grandfather with musket in hand leaving their rural home to join their comrades in battle. Needless to say, apparently there are several different versions of this painting, too.

Bedford Hist. Soc.

Coach and Horses (A-13) Circa 1880
Willard's smallest work (3⅛" x 5")
(Bedford Historical Society)

W.F.G.

Dog (A-17) 1880
(W.R.H.S.)

TAKING THE BULL BY THE HORNS.

J.F. RYDER, Cleveland, O.

(H.M.L.)

H.M.L.

Willard at the height of his career. Circa 1890's.

61

United we stand—divided we fall (A-57) Circa 1875
A political moral cartoon told in humorous form.

THE DANITES.

MARRIED MUM ?   NO SIR!

The Danites (A-54)
The joyous effect of a single woman on the morale of the men in a Western town.

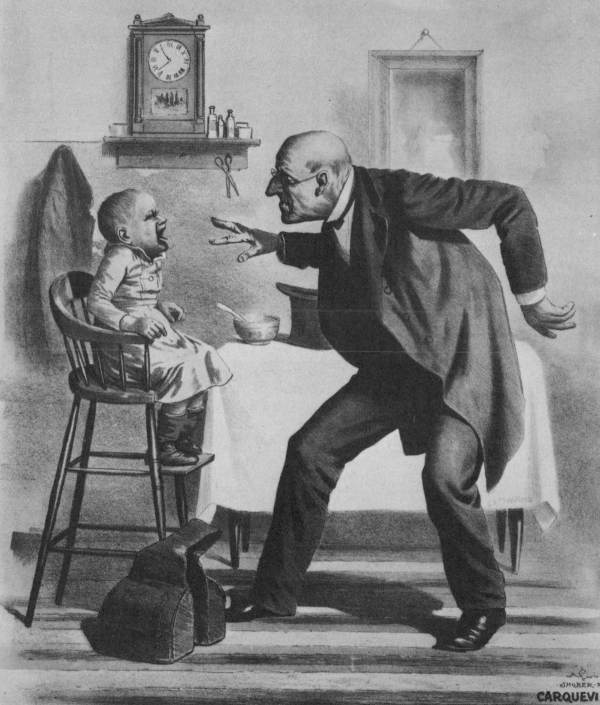

Book Illustration (A-58)   (Library of Congress)

H.M.L.

Barton's Ancestor (A-85)   (Barton Family/photo H.M.L.)
Painted for Rev. W. Barton, Willard's minister and close friend. According to the Barton legend, during the Revolutionary War, the Barton ancestor was drawing water from the river when accosted by a British officer on horseback. Barton knocked the officer from his horse with a swing of the bucket, seized the officer's sword and swam across the river to join the American Revolutionary Forces.

W.F.G.

Christmas (A-5) 1881   (W.R.H.S.)
Poor girl stares in wonderment at Christmas stocking.

W.F.G.

Shaker Elder (P-25) Circa 1887   (W.R.H.S.)

"When, in the course of human events it becomes necessary—"

Political Lithographs (A-55 & A-56), copyrighted by J. F. Ryder, depicting the change in American-English relationships in 1776 and 1876.

Why bless my heart Johnny, you're Welcome! How's your mother?

What Columbus Found (A-16) 1892
Columbus and his soldiers discover the inhabitants of the "New World."

A.M.Willard

Drummer's Last Yarn (A-1) 1885
Traveling salesman telling "shady" story. Note scornful look of lady behind and to left of drummer. Posed by members of the Willard family.

(Stouffer Foods Corp.)

Vixseboxse Galleries, Cle.

68

CREATION
Assuming the Burden of Greatness.

Real Cause of all the Trouble Illustrated by the Pencil of Willard.

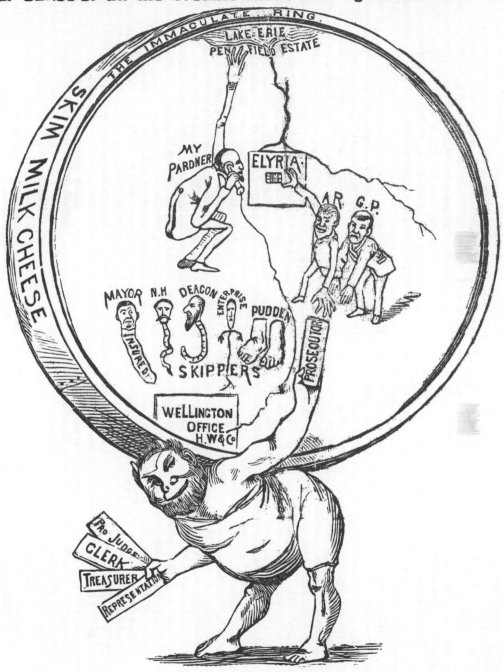

This cartoon appeared in an Elyria, Ohio newspaper on October 10, 1884—The political involvement of Milk & Cheese interests in Northern Ohio.
(H.M.L.)

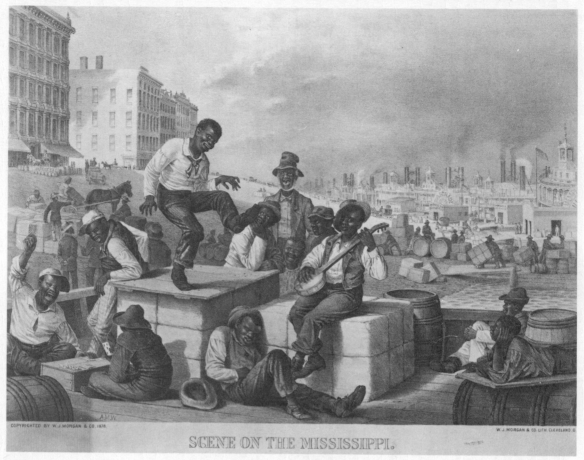

Scene on the Mississippi (A-53)
Dock workers, circa 1878.

Lake Scene (L-19)
(W.R.H.S.)

Father Come Home (A-7)
Willard's sensitivity to the social issues of the times.
(W.R.H.S.)

The Sketch Book, 1883

These caricatures, typical of Willard graffiti, are excerpts from "Views in the Holy Land of Chautauqua." Similar sketches appeared on most any surface that would sustain Willard's artistic efforts, including fences, walls, and the backs of filing cabinets.

A-80

(Cleveland Public Library)

GRANDMA'S CHAIR,

A-79 (Cleveland Public Library)

Sketchbook, 1883

The artist, with young model, possibly his grandson, Willard Connally. A vast number of Willard paintings fill the walls.

THE GOLDEN YEARS—1895-1918

The Golden Years were times for remembering family, old friends, old places, and old paintings.

Willard was ill through most of the early winter of 1896-1897. By February he had recovered sufficiently to travel to Florida where he visited with old Wellington friends. The warm weather and balmy sea breezes restored his health, and soon his canvas was filled with seascapes and local sketches.

His last major humorous work, **Pitching the Tune,** was completed later that year. It showed an old-fashioned choir led by a director who with tuning fork to ear, is giving the choir their pitch.

Most of Willard's family modeled for the choir members. A local ditch digger was recruited to model for the minister, and much to his astonishment, he received $5.00 per pose, "Just to set and take it easy."[65]

The Spirit of '76 was Willard's greatest triumph. He instinctively returned to this work, creating not only the large Cleveland City Hall replica but the numerous oils and watercolors for friends and relatives.

Nellie died in 1912, and Willard's daughter, Maud, and her son, Willard Connally, moved into the artist's home in Cleveland, the grandson to model, not only as the new "young drummer boy," but also for canvases on other themes.

In 1915, Archibald traveled west to visit his nephew, Theodore Arthur (T.A.) Willard, in California. The artist completed many landscapes of the scenic west, including several of the Grand Canyon. T.A. arranged for motion picture footage of Willard and these paintings at Universal Studios.

World War I renewed interest in the **Spirit of**

W.F.G.

Self Portrait III (P-3)   (W.R.H.S.)

(H.M.L.)   J. F. Ryder Studio

Comparison of Willard self portrait and Ryder photograph
around the turn of the century.

Willard's face appears quite often in this later period. There was a third self portrait—he is included as one of the **Three Men Talking** and he appears as a subject in his two versions of the **Battle of San Juan Hill**.. a group of veterans in a retirement home.

An additional patriotic work, **Battle of Concord Bridge** was completed about 1898.

'76 and Willard himself. He was often called upon to ride in parades, usually following three men dressed as his famous marching drum and fife trio.

He lauded America for its entry into the war to liberate humanity. He expressed confidence that the American Flag, which he loved, would return from France with new glories of victory.

H.M.L.

Pitching the Tune (A-21) 1894
Posed by the Willard family and a ditch digger.

H.M.L.

The Politicians/Three men talking (A-6)
Willard modeled for the man on right. (W.R.H.S.)

The Battle of San Juan Hill (A-8) 1907 (W.R.H.S.)
Willard modeled for man center, with pool cue. A second version was painted including only the seven central figures.

A.M.Willard

76

Grand Canyon (L-17)   (W.R.H.S.)

Willard was a familiar figure in Cleveland, now stoop-shouldered, with black felt hat and cape. He made frequent trips to Wellington where he signed and dated many of his earlier paintings owned by old friends. As his strength and hand weakened, he personally colored and signed photographs and lithographs of his **Spirit of '76**.

About a year before his death, he told T.A. Willard he felt his usefulness was about over and that life held but little of interest to him. T. A. requested he take one of his sketches of the view of the mountains and valley in Provo, Utah, and complete it in oil for him. It was Willard's last major work.

He died on October 11, 1918, and was buried in the family plot in the Greenwood Cemetery in Wellington. His old friend, Reverend William Barton officiated at the services. One of the Cleveland papers printed the following obituary—

> "It may be that the late A. M. Willard was not a great painter. He lacked training; he lacked opportunities, but his work was filled with an inspiration that overshadowed technical skill. His one great effort—great in originality, in sincerity, in heart appeal, stood out among American paintings, . . . It became the best known picture in our country . . ."[66]

AFTER WILLARD'S DEATH—1918 to Date

The artist's wife and four of his six children preceded him in death. Son Harry died in 1917. Of the remaining two children, Maud died in 1922, and Byron in 1936. Willard's daughter, Maud, provided him with his only grandchild,

Willard Connally. Connally left no heirs—Archibald M. Willard's line had come to an end.

Of the three principal figures in the **Spirit of '76**, Reverend Samuel Willard died in 1876, and Hugh Mosher in 1892. The young drummer boy, Henry K. Devereux, died in 1932.

For a number of years, son Byron Willard was the family spokesman and authority on "Arch" Willard. He was aided by his cousin, John J. Thomas, Jr. Through the 1920's and early 1930's, Thomas became a Willard zealot. According to Robert L. Walden, Wellington historian,

> "The evangelistic efforts of John J. Thomas, Jr. through his published statements, addresses and especially through the publication and distribution of tens of thousands of large prints of the **Spirit of '76**, acted as stimuli to keep Willard's fame alive."[67]

Thomas, along with another nephew, Dr. Ben Colver, and assisted by Ben Wickham, Cleveland lawyer and long time friend of the Willard family, acquired a large collection of Willard paintings, at one time estimated to include some 100 different works. Thomas spent one summer in Wellington negotiating to establish a Willard museum. His preferred location was an addition to the Herrick Memorial Library. Again, according to Walden,

> "This project like all of the other ones came to naught. He left his native village and never returned."[68]

W.F.G.

Willard Family Memorial, Wellington

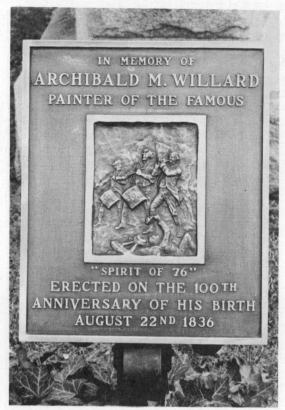

IN MEMORY OF
ARCHIBALD M. WILLARD
PAINTER OF THE FAMOUS

"SPIRIT OF 76"
ERECTED ON THE 100TH
ANNIVERSARY OF HIS BIRTH
AUGUST 22ND 1836

W.F.G.

not only at the Herrick Memorial Library, but also at the Southern Lorain County Historical Society. The Herrick Library collection contains the **Fourth of July Cartoon,** the early **Charcoal Sketch,** the Barton gift, **Spirit of '76,** many of Willard's early Wellington children's portraits, humorous paintings and early Wellington landscapes.

Mr. Ernst Henes, one time editor and publisher of the "Wellington Enterprise" and long time Willard supporter, was principally responsible for the establishment of the Southern Lorain County Historical Society. Special emphasis has been placed on Willard paintings and memorabilia.

Mr. Ernst Henes

For the most part, Willard's paintings were passed from family to family. It has been fairly easy to keep track of those with close ties to the Cleveland or Wellington areas. Unfortunately a great number of his canvases are lost or missing. I now have cataloged some 200 different works, and feel it is only a small part of his total effort.

In 1936, an attempt was made to list Willard's paintings in preparation for a Willard display at the Great Lakes Exposition. In addition to the Thomas Collection, a Miss Ethel Quinlan had also acquired a number of Willard's paintings. Her collection was loaned to the Western Reserve Historical Society in June, 1936. The following November, Willard Connally borrowed a number of these paintings. It is not known what further negotiations, if any, occurred between Miss Quinlan and Willard Connally, because Connally never returned the paintings, and eventually gave or willed them to his friends.

Over the years, the Western Reserve Historical Society has gathered a sizeable collection of Willard's works including the two-thirds size Ryder's gift, **Spirit of '76,** 2 water colors of the **Spirit of '76,** the **Drummer Hand Studies,** 2 self-portraits, and many Americana themes as well as landscapes.

The other main Willard center is the Wellington area where collections are located

WELLINGTON
"THE SPIRIT OF '76"
PAINTED BY
ARCHIBALD M.
WILLARD
WHO LIVED HERE

W.F.G.

Another smaller Willard collection is stored by Mr. Alden Hare of Cleveland, a close boyhood friend of Willard Connally and neighbor of the artist. Hare has been most active in veterans and civic affairs, stressing the **Spirit of '76** theme. Additionally, he has been actively seeking support for a Willard Museum in Cleveland, to not only honor Willard, but other leading Cleveland figures as well.

Smaller Willard collections are also located at the Geauga County Historical Society in Burton, Ohio, and the Bedford Historical Society in Bedford, Ohio.

The City of Cleveland's 8' by 10' **Spirit of '76** is located in the Cleveland City Hall. Marblehead's 8' by 10' **Spirit of '76** is located in the Board of Selectmen's room in the town's Abbot Hall. They also have an early Willard self portrait, and a late portrait of Willard by the artist Frank H. Tompkins.

On June 14, 1932, Byron Willard unveiled a plaque marking the site of the Willis Adams studio. It read:

"ON THIS SITE IN A FOURTH FLOOR STUDIO ARCHIBALD M. WILLARD IN 1876 PAINTED **THE SPIRIT OF '76.**"

In 1936, the Great Lakes exhibition in Cleveland featured Willard's paintings. At that time, Willard Park was dedicated just east of Cleveland City Hall.

In 1937, a Bill was introduced in the United States Senate to appropriate $250,000 to erect a bronze replica of the **Spirit of '76** in Willard Park. Evidently no action was taken.

On July 3, 1955, the town of Bedford, Ohio, erected a bronze tablet memorializing Willard. The plaque was attached to a 20-ton boulder in the park across from the site of the Bedford First Baptist Church which was founded by Reverend Samuel Willard in 1834.

Spirit of '76 drums are located at both the Bedford Historical Society and the Southern Lorain County Historical Society. Hugh Mosher's fifes have remained in the family—one, until recently was played at Wellington functions by his great grandson, Horace B. McClafflin.

Significant Willard publications include

Willard Memorial . Bedford. Ohio

Bedford Historical Society

Devereux's book, **The Spirit of '76,** 1926; a delightful children's book, **Yankee Doodle Painter,** 1955, by Anne Colver, a Willard great-niece; Robert L. Walden's series on Willard in the "Wellington Enterprise;" and Arthur H. Auten's Masters thesis on Willard, Western Reserve University, 1960.

The Willard Family Association, whose members trace their American heritage to the year 1634, are especially proud of "Arch" Willard. The annual family Association meeting was held in Wellington in 1967, and is scheduled again for 1976. The members were most active in supporting the **Spirit of '76** Bicentennial commemorative postage stamp.

Ray LaMacchia, President New Spirit/Wellington Committee, presents portfolio of "Wellington Collection" Willard lithographs to President Gerald Ford, July 1975.

Special recognition must be given to Ray LaMacchia, president of the New Spirit/ Wellington Committee, currently giving added exposure to Willard's work, coordinating exhibitions through the National Endowment for the Arts, and the Lorain County and Ohio Arts Councils. The Diamond Shamrock Corporation whose world headquarters are located in Cleveland, has most graciously sponsored the "Wellington Collection," a traveling Bicentennial exhibition of Willard's paintings.

CHAPTER IV

Lost Willard Paintings

Help Sought in Locating Lost Willard Paintings

Over the years a great number of Willard's works have been lost or misplaced. Fortunately we have descriptions of some of these canvases, and it is hoped, that through proper exposure, a number of them might be relocated.

I would estimate that the Catalogue Raisonne' covers only a small portion of Willard's total effort. Of these listings, nearly one half of them are missing.

Where we have references to lithographs, or humorous reproductions, there might possibly be original oil or water-color paintings. In many cases where there are known paintings, Ryder possibly reproduced them by lithograph—the lithographs, in many cases, are collectors items in themselves.

The Spirit of '76 was Willard's favorite work. There were many related paintings, especially studies of Hugh Mosher. Several of these are missing. Willard created several sculptures, one of

Pluck II (PL-2-II)   (Stouffer Foods Corp.)
One of Willard's many Pluck replicas. This version was stolen from the Stouffer's Restaurant in Washington, D.C. in the mid 1960's.

H.M.L.

Hugh Mosher (P-27)   (Photo H.M.L.)
An example of Willard art that has been photographed, but contact lost with the painting itself.

The Spirit of '76 trio, one of **The Old Drummer,** modeled by his father, Rev. Samuel Willard. Both of these are missing. Additionally Willard created many small water color detail studies of the **Spirit of '76.** Two **Old Drummer Hand Studies,** 8½'' x 7'', are at the Western Reserve Historical Society. Others of a similar style and size were borrowed by a Cleveland Newspaper in the 1930's.

Willard created many replicas of his favorite works. This occurred not only in **The Spirit of '76,** but in his children's **Pluck 1 & 2.** In addition there were variations on the Pluck theme as seen in "Bees" and the illustrations for Barton's book, "The Story of a Pumpkin Pie." He even repeated landscapes, and portraits, not to mention his other patriotic and humorous works. Most important of all, I feel we will still find more **Spirit of '76** canvases in time.

Willard decorated many churches, public buildings, and prominent homes in the Northern Ohio area from the late 1870's through 1900, while working under contract for Max Cook. It included murals, frescos and vignettes. He usually left some form of signature.

Example of his work may be seen at the Western Reserve Historical Society in Cleveland, The Herrick Memorial Library and the Southern Lorain County Historical Society in Wellington,

Trotting Horse about to be sold (A-2)

A "Lost Treasure" recently found patching a hole in a Bedford barn wall. Restored, it exemplifies Willard's early technique. Many similar works still lie, unknown or forgotten, in other barns, sheds, attics or basements, especially in the Northern Ohio area.　　　　　　　　　　　　(Edward B. Stvan Col.)

and smaller collections seen at the Geauga Co. Historical Society in Burton, and The Bedford Historical Society, Bedford.

Most of the lost Willard art will be located in Northern Ohio, especially for those with connections to Cleveland, Bedford, or Wellington. Many have been handed down from family to family, many delegated to attic or rummage sale. **Trotting Horse About To Be Sold**, once covered a hole in a Bedford barn wall. The giant 10′ x 12′ **Allegorical Birth of the Flag**, once served as a waterproof cover.

It is important to cross-reference paintings by title, medium, size, signature, date, etc., as listed in the Catalogue Raisonne.' The librarian at the Herrick Memorial Library, Wellington, Ohio, 44090, will coordinate authentication referrals and records.

LOST PAINTINGS

Early newspaper accounts provide the following descriptions:

1. **A Little Fishing Incident,** (A-38), humorous, circa 1878, "a small boy is seated on the bank of a small stream dangling his line in the shallow water. A companion lies behind him on the grass, while a bright little girl, with whose merry smiles the sunlight of the picture mingles, is slyly reaching with a small stick to push the young angler's hat over his eyes, while he is plainly losing his temper and meditating a thrashing for his innocent companion, whom he suspects of the annoyance."

2. **Canal Lock,** (A-39), pastoral, circa 1878, "the scene is a Canal Lock, where a boat is about to enter, and under the spreading tree upon the bank, some children watch the boatman's movements. Under the branches the view extends across the fields to the distant village while overhead the sky is striped with light clouds. The cool shade which is represented in the foreground contrasts with the bright sunshine which breaks through the scudding clouds upon the distant fields."

3. **Spring & Autumn** (A-40), a pair of paintings, circa 1879, "The principal feature of these pictures is the landscape which is unusually natural."

4. **Venus** (A-10), circa 1875, sold to Dr. F. N. Clark, Dentist, Euclid Ave., Cle., on Dec. 4, 1875.

5. **General Garfield**, (P-32), portrait, circa 1881, "a large picture of General Garfield at Chickamauga " Willard also created a sculpture, **Bust of General Garfield** (SC-1) that was highly acclaimed in 1886.

6. **Winter Sports**, (A-41), humorous, circa 1881, "the central figure is an elderly gentleman, once of great dignity. He has been caught between two opposing parties of boys and has received the benefit of their snowballs, which rather destroys his stateliness and stove pipe hat. The passers-by enjoy the fun immensely."

7. **A View On The Southern Mississippi,** (A-89), Americana, circa 1881, "a steam boat in the river, a family group under a tree in the left, and a party of cotton pickers in a field in the right foreground."

8. **The Origin of the American Flag,** (A-9b), Patriotic, circa 1876, (30″ x 40″).(Note: a 10′ x 12′ version of this painting is at the Western Reserve Hist. Soc., Cle.) Left to Right: Christopher Columbus, Martin Luther (with hand raised), and George Washington standing on a hill. "The origin of the National flag was represented by alternate bars of blue and glowing red, as seen in the sky at dawn by the reflection of the first light of day upon the wavy lines of summer clouds with the stars of early morning intermingled against the blue background."

9. **The Battle of Concord Bridge**, (A-45), patriotic, circa 1859, painted for the Colonial Club, Cleveland.

10. **John Hay,** (P-44), Portrait, "aide-de-camp and assistant private secretary to President Lincoln, and author of one of Lincoln's biographies,

A 1926 Exhibition of Willard Art—nearly all now lost or missing. A photograph of the window display of Willard Art in the Guardian Trust Bank of Cleveland, around 1926, plainly shows (left to right), the missing Head of Hugh Mosher (P-27); the missing "Spirit of '76," painted for Willard's lawyer Fred Friend; a pair of Plucks, the second painting was stolen from Stouffer's Restaurant in Washington, D.C.; and one of the three missing replicas of Jim Bludso.

83

and later Secretary of State under Presidents McKinley and Roosevelt."

11. **Prehistoric Dinosaurs**, (A-36), circa 1872, approx. 5' x 15', painted for a visiting lecturer, dark blue colors, drab and not especially attractive. Purchased by Wm. Vischer.

Names of paintings, with no description:

12. **Lake Erie** (A-19)
13. **The Fire** (A-20)
14. **The Buggy Shop** (A-25)
15. **Arabian Girl** (A-26)
16. **Going Home** (A-43), circa 1894
17. **What Are The Wild Waves Saying** (A-90)
18. **Scoot Brother Scoot** (A-91)
19. **Ouch** (A-86)
20. **Before The Boom** (A-87)
21. **After the Boom** (A-88)
22. **Ashtabula Valley** (L-23)
23. **Black River** (L-24)
24. **Southern Scene** (L-28)
25. **Sketches of Florida Coast** (L-58)

In 1936, a list of Willard's works was prepared for the art display at the Great Lakes Exposition. Over the ensuing 40 years, contact has been lost with the owners of these paintings.

26. **Drummers Last Yarn**, (A-1), U. Needs, Cle.
27. **Boy Stung by Bees**, (A-23a), J. R. Brennan. Cle.
28. **Aunt Fat and Aunt Lean**, (A-24a), Water Color, (12"x18"), Two Negro Women, John Kiffer, Cle.
29. **Minuteman** (A-12), Gilmore Knights of Columbus
30. **The Scout** (A-48), Water Color, (6" x 8"), Army Scout on plains, with Red Shirt, Dr. Wm Ridel, Cle.
31. **Barbara Fritchie** (Lithograph) (A-52)
32. **Creek**, Landscape (L-30), 12" x 16", Kenneth Sifert, Cle.
33. **Old Mill Dam and Mill**, (L-31), landscape, Water Color, (10" x 14"), Kenneth Sifert, Cle.
34. **Valley of Aurora Branch, Chagrin River** (L-32), landscape oil, circa 1900, C.A. Rock, Cle.
35. **Rural Farm Scene**, (L-33) Landscape, oil (24"x36"), circa 1872, Henry D. Parsons, Homestead, small figures.
36. **Pluck**, (Pair), owned by James Brennan, Mrs. Byron Willard, John J. Thomas.
37. **Mrs. Edwards**, (P-36) portrait, Mrs. Geo. Richardson.
38. **Mr. Townsend** (P-38), portrait, head and shoulders in oval, charcoal, (24" x 30"), Robert Townsend.

Miss Ethel Quinlan acquired a sizeable collection of Willard paintings. Most of these were donated to the Western Reserve Historical Society, others, however, are still missing.

39. **Maud Connally**, portrait, artist's daughter, (P-14)
40. **"Brother"**, Portrait of Artist's Brother, (P-15)
41. **"Son?"** Portrait of artist's son (P-16)
42. **Still Life: Fruit** (A-50)
43. **Farm Scene**, (L14) Landscape, pond at right, Unsigned, (20" x 30")

Willard Connally, the artist's grandson, borrowed some of Miss Quinlan's collection. It is believed he gave some of these paintings to his friends.

44. **Provo Canyon**, (L-35), landscape, unsigned, (12¼" x 18½")
45. **Rural Scene** (L-36), landscape: bridge to left, cottage to center and right, unsigned, (11¼" x 18½")
46. **Forest Scene**, (L-37) Landscape, Fallen tree at right, signed, (12¼" x 18½")
47. **Fall Scene**, (L-40), landscape, trees on bank in background, signed, (12 ¼" x 18½")
48. **Landscape** (L-41), Tree in center, unsigned, (12¼" x 18½")
49. **Fire Scene** (A-49), Group of people at a fire, unsigned, (12¼" x 18½")
50. **Rural Scene**, landscape (L-39), with road and bridge across stream (12¼" x 18½")
51. **Tropical Scene**, (L-38) landscape with palm trees, unsigned, (12¼" x 18½")

The following works have been described from memory:

52. **Euclid Ave** (A-14), Winter scene on Euclid Ave., Cle.
53. **Dog, Lying Down** (A-18), not signed, shown to Cle. art dealer in early 1960's.
54. **Shaker Family** (A-42), Shaker family in living room, circa 1887
55. **Head of Hugh Mosher** (P-28), the fifer, seen in Cle. in 1960's

Although some information is known on the location of the following paintings, further information would be of assistance.

56. **Cornelia's Jewels** (A-78), Roman Matron & her sons, water color, small;
57. **Pitching the Tune** Dr. Ben Colver, Los Angeles, 1936 (A-21)
58. **Bald Mountain, Utah,** Landscape, Clarance Willard, 1936 (L-34)
59. **Wayside Landscape,** H. H. Fisher to Ernest Root. (L-61)
60. **Dog & Parrot**, (A-46) Wm Vischer
61. **Jim Bludso** (A-51) Copies for Agda Thomas, John Hay, Wm Walter Phelps.
62. **Aztec Sacrifice** (A-27) circa 1917, Southwest Museum, Los Angeles
63. **The Tramps** (A-47) oil, Evelyn Artz
64. **Barton's Ancestor**, (A-85), Photo at H.M.L., Wellington
65. **Landscape** (L-54) Evelyn Artz

This catalogue will be in a constant state of revision.

Over the years a great number of Willard's works have been lost or misplaced. Contact must be re-established with the owners.

A good deal of the information included herein is inaccurate, incomplete, or unknown. Corrections and additions are solicited.

Please verify all comments by catalogue classification and number, checking medium, signature, size, date, and ownership. Willard duplicated many of his works in all classifications.

Forward all correspondence to A. M. Willard Files, Herrick Memorial Library, Wellington, Ohio 44090.

CLASSIFICATIONS

SP —Spirit(s) of '76
CW—Civil War
 A—Americana
PL—Pluck
 P—Portraits
 L—Landscapes
 M—Murals
SC—Sculpture

"Oil"—Oil on canvas, unless otherwise stated.

OWNERSHIP CODES

W.R.H.S. — Western Reserve Historical Society, Cleveland, Ohio

H.M.L.   — Herrick Memorial Library, Wellington, Ohio

S.L.H.S. — Southern Lorain County Historical Society, Wellington, Ohio

SPIRIT(S) OF '76

SP-1 Fourth of July Musicians Cartoon: Ink Drawing: 13½''x17½'': Signed, ''A. M. Willard'': Not Dated: Redrawing of the original cartoon at the suggestion of Rev. Wm. Barton in 1895. Autographed to Rev. Barton. Barton to H.M.L. (Original Cartoon Lost)

SP-2 Preliminary Sketch: Crayon Drawing: 18''x24'': Signed and Dated, ''A. M. Willard/1876'': Wm. Sawtelle to Rev. Wm. Barton to H.M.L.

SP-3 Lithographer's Small Oil: (Missing ?): Oil: Approx. 18''x24'': Circa 1875: (Note: A small oil, 19''x25'', nearly identical to the lithograph, not signed or dated, pending authentication, Hemingway Galleries, Jamestown, New York)

SP-4 Design For a Painting: Sketch: Circa 1875: Inscribed "Yankee Doodle," left side, and "J. F. Ryder, Proprietor," right side. Library of Congress No. 11242 (1926).

SP-5 Centennial Canvas: (Missing): Oil: 8'x10': Signed, ''A. M. Willard'': Possibly not dated. Completed 1876: Lost or overpainted.

SP-6 Cleveland Gray's: (Missing): Oil: 8'x13': Unknown signature or date, completed 1877: Lost or overpainted, possibly at Marblehead (SP-7).

SP-7 Marblehead (Devereux's Purchase): Oil: Approx. 8'x10': Signed and Dated, ''A. M. Willard/1876'': Repainted by Willard in 1892, older painting underneath. Devereux donated to Abbot Hall, Marblehead, Mass.

SP-8 Western Reserve Historical Society (Ryder's Gift): Oil: 4'4''x6'10'': Signed ''A. M. Willard'': Not Dated, completed 1895: Painted for J. F. Ryder. Ryder to Bowersox to W.R.H.S.: W.R.H.S. No. 40.1349.

SP-9 Thomas Gift: Oil: 3'x4': Signed, ''A. M. Willard'': Not Dated, completed 1912: Wedding Gift to Willard's Nephew, John J. Thomas, Jr. Thomas to L. L. Bucklew to Willard Gordon to Metromedia, Inc. (On Freedom Train).

SP-10 Cleveland Commission: Oil: 8'x10': Not Signed or Dated, Completed in 1913. Cleveland City Hall.

SP-11 Herrick Memorial Library (Barton Gift): Oil: 28''x34'': Signed and Dated, ''A. M. Willard/1916'': Gift for Rev. W. Barton. Barton to H.M.L.

SP-12 Water Color No. 1 (Willard Family): Water Color: 19½″x23″: Signed and Dated, "A. M. Willard/1916": T. A. Willard to Alfred R. Willard to W.R.H.S.: W.R.H.S. No. 68.1.1.

SP-13 Water Color No. 2 (Dr. Wilfred Sharp): Water Color: 17½″x23″: Signed "A. M. Willard": Not Dated, Circa 1916. Dr. Sharp to W.R.H.S. W.R.H.S. No. 47.3.

SP-14 Fred Friend Gift: (Missing): Oil: Approx. 19″x22″: Signed and Dated, "A. M. Willard/1876": Probably painted 1910's: Gift to Willard's lawyer, Fred Friend. Similar to Marblehead.

SP-15 On to Havana: (Missing): Sketch: Unknown size: Signed "A. M. Willard": Not Dated, Circa 1898. Spanish-American War Version, printed in "Cleveland Plain Dealer," May 15, 1898.

SP-16 Spirit of '76 Vases: (2) Pair of Vases painted by Willard: Jim Diamond.

SPIRIT OF '76 DETAIL STUDIES

SP-101 Old Drummer Right Hand: Water Color: 7″x8½″: Not Signed or Dated: Harry Willard to Alfred R. Willard to W.R.H.S. W.R.H.S. No. 68.1.2.

SP-102 Old Drummer Left Hand: Water Color: 7″x8½″: Not Signed or Dated: Harry Willard to Alfred R. Willard to W.R.H.S.: W.R.H.S. No. 68.1.3.

CIVIL WAR

CW-1 Battle of Cumberland Gap No. 1: (Missing): Sketch: Size Unknown: Not Signed or Dated, Circa 1863: Photo of Sketch at H.M.L. (Line of soldiers marching across hill).

CW-2 Battle of Cumberland Gap No. 2: (Missing): Sketch: Size Unknown: Not Signed or Dated, Circa 1863: Photo of sketch at H.M.L. (View of farm valley from hilltop).

CW-3 Civil War Panorama: (Destroyed by artist): Oil: 6′x12′, Scenes on canvas 100 yards long. Circa 1863-1865.

AMERICANA

A-1 Drummer's Last Yarn: Oil: Approx. 3′x4′: Signed and Dated, "A. M. Willard/1885": U. S. Needs 1936 to Stouffer Foods Corp. (Traveling salesman telling "shady story" to group in railroad car.)

A-2 Trotting Horse About to be Sold: Oil: 42″x-30″: Signed and Dated, "Willard/1867": Yoder to E. Stvan (Rural scene: Several persons examining horse and surrey).

A-3 The Awkward Squad: Oil on Wood: 8″x-10″: Not Signed or Dated, Circa 1865: H. Devereux to W.R.H.S.: W.R.H.S. No. 2007 (Civil War sergeant addressing two awkward recruits).

A-4a Deacon Jones' Experience: Oil (Sepia): 30″x20″: Signed, "A. M. Willard" (Signed Twice): Not Dated, Circa 1873: W. J. Hunkin to W.R.H.S. W.R.H.S. 1931. (Family kneeling in living room in prayer—dog has chased cat upon father's back to amusement of rest of family.)

A-4b Deacon Jones' Experience: Oil on Wood: Graff to Hare.

A-4c Deacon Jones' Experience: Allen Art Museum, Oberlin, Ohio.

A-5 Christmas: Oil: 16″x22″: Signed and Dated, "A. M. Willard/1881": Mary Chandler to Robert Chandler to W.R.H.S.: W.R.H.S. No. 57.201 (Poor girl stares in wonder at her lone stocking hung on fireplace.)

A-6 The Politicians: Oil: 36″x26″: Signed "A. M. Willard": Not Dated, Circa 1910: W. Sharp to W.R.H.S.: W.R.H.S. No. 47.4 (Three men talking animatedly—Willard on Rt.)

A-7 Father Come Home: Oil: 30″x27¼″: Signed and Dated on back of canvas, "A. M. Willard/1878": Ethel Quinlan to W.R.H.S.: W.R.H.S. No. 42.121 (Poor barefoot girl trying to persuade father to leave saloon.)

A-8a Battle of San Juan Hill: Oil: 44½″x32½″: Signed and Dated, "A. M. Willard/1907": W. Sharp to W.R.H.S.: W.R.H.S. No. 47.5 (Spanish-American War veterans in "Old Soldiers Home" discussing news—Willard in center with pool cue.)

A-8b Battle of San Juan Hill: Oil: 29½″x21½″: Signed "A. M. Willard": Not Dated: Graff to H.M.L. (Same as A-8a, but with smaller grouping of men.)

A-9a Allegorical Birth of the Flag: Oil: 10′x12′: Not Signed or Dated, Circa 1878: Lattimer to Cleveland Art Museum to W.R.H.S.: W.R.H.S. No. 59.1012 (Columbus, George Washington and Martin Luther stand on hill as setting sun displays colors of the flag in the sky.)

A-9b Allegorical Birth of the Flag: (Missing): Probably Oil: 30″x40″: Unknown signature or date, Circa 1877.

A-10 Venus: (Missing): Oil: Circa 1875: Dr. F. N. Clark, 1875.

A-11 Roman Prisoner: Oil: 30″x35″: Signed "A. Willard": Not Dated, Circa 1874: Dr. F. N. Clark 1875, Graff to H.M.L. (Manacled prisoner strains at chains.)

A-12 Minutemen: Oil: 35″x49½″: Signed "A. M. Willard": Not Dated, Circa 1890's: F. N. Iamarino (Revolutionary War family in foreground—Minutemen and Red Coats in background.)

A-13 Coach & Horses: Oil: 3″x5″: Not Signed or Dated, Circa 1880: A. Wackerman to Bedford Historical Society. (Four horses draw coach with passengers.)

A-14 Euclid Ave.: (Missing): Oil: (Early) (Winter scene on Euclid Ave., Cleveland.)

A-15 Minutemen of the Revolution: Oil: 8′x6′: Signed and Dated, "A. M. Willard/1888": The Union Club, Cleveland. (Family in front of rural home—father and grandfather prepare to leave for Revolutionary War battle.)

A-16 What Columbus Found: Lithograph: Signed "A. M. Willard": Published by J. F. Ryder 1892: Library of Congress. (Columbus and two soldiers look through bushes and see Indians playing baseball.)

A-17 Dog (Standing): Oil: 10″x13″: Signed and Dated, "A.M.W./1880": J. F. Ryder to Mary Graff to W.R.H.S.: W.R.H.S. No. 3758. (Back view of dog standing on steps.)

A-18 Dog (Lying Down): (Missing): Oil: Small: Not Signed: Seen in Cleveland, 1963.

A-19 Lake Erie: (Missing): Oil: Listed in "Cleveland Plain Dealer" 1936.

A-20 The Fire: (Missing): Oil: Listed in "Cleveland Plain Dealer", 1936.

A-21 Pitching the Tune: Oil: Est. 2′x3′: Signed and Dated, "A. M. Willard/1894", Circa 1895: Dr. Ben Colver, 1936. (Country choir, posed by Willard Family.)

A-22 Two Figures Roadside Conversation: Oil: 15″x12″: Signed "A. M. Willard": Not Dated, Circa 1868: E. G. Fisher to Ed Wells. (Man on tired white horse, talking to Negro man, in black top hat, sitting on tree stump—town in background.)

A-23a Boy Stung by Bees: (Missing): Oil: J. R. Brennan, Cle. 1936.

A-23b Bees: Oil: 30″x25″: Signed "AWillard": Not Dated, Circa 1875: T. Herrick to Mrs. D. Arnold to H.M.L. (Farm Scene: two boys and a girl being stung by bees.)

A-24a Aunt Fat and Autie Lean: (Missing): Water Color: 12″x18″: Unknown signature and date: John Kiffer, Cleveland, 1936. (Two Negro women; fat one sitting in rocking chair, thin one standing.)

A-24b Jenny Fry and Sister Johnson: (Probably same as 24a.)

A-25 Buggy Shop: (Missing)

A-26 Arabian Girl: (Missing)

A-27 Aztec Sacrifice: (Missing): Oil: Unknown Size, Signature or Date, Circa 1917: T. A. Willard to Southwest Museum, Los Angeles, 1945. (Mayan Indian sacrifice—Indian tied to rock altar, about to be killed.) Note: T. A. Willard, Archeologist in Central America, and nephew of artist.

A-28 Women's Rights: Lithograph: 4¼″x6½″: H.M.L. (Wife sits by fire reading, while older woman, her mother or housekeeper, stands nearby reading paper, husband holds crying baby, second baby cries in its cradle.)

A-29 Oh, Brigham—How Could You Leave Us?: Lithograph: 4¼″x6½″: Signed "A. M. Willard": H.M.L. (Funeral mourners.)

A-30 A Tail I Could Unfold: Lithograph: 4¼″x6½″: Not Signed: H.M.L. (Little girl with big turkey.)

A-31 The Missing Link: Lithograph: 4¼″x6½″: Not Signed: H.M.L. (Man arguing with butcher while holding sausages behind his back.)

A-32 Picturesque Africa: Lithograph: 4¼″x6½″: Not Signed: H.M.L. (Man laughing, holding baby in his lap.)

A-33 In This Wheat Rye and Bye: Lithograph: 4¼″x6½″: Not signed: H.M.L. (Two grasshoppers on farm fence—one playing an accordian, both singing.)

A-34 What is Home Without a Mother?: Lithograph: 4¼″x6½″: Not signed: H.M.L. (Mother spanks child with hairbrush—overturned preserve jar lies on floor.)

A-35 **Taking the Bull by the Horns**: Lithograph: 4¼″x6½″: Not Signed: H.M.L. (Bull chases two men who are jumping over fence.)

A-36 **Dinosaur**: (Missing): Oil: Est. 5′x15′: Unknown Signature or Date, Circa 1872: Prepared for visiting lecturer on "Marvels of the Natural World." Purchased by Wm. Vischer.

A-37 **A Bird in the Hand is Worth Two in the Bush**: Lithograph: 4¼″x6½″: Not signed: H.M.L. (Man sneaking out of chicken coop with lantern in one hand, chicken in other hand.)

A-38 **A Little Fishing Incident**: (Missing): Oil: Unknown Size, Signature or Date, Circa 1878. Listed "Cleveland Herald" August 26, 1878. (Two boys fishing—one boy wrongly hits other when girl pushes hat over his eyes.)

A-39 **Canal Lock**: (Missing): Oil: Unknown Size, Signature or Date, Circa 1878. Listed "Cleveland Herald" Sept. 19, 1878. (Children watching canal boat enter lock.)

A-40 **Spring & Autumn** (Pair): (Missing): Oil: Unknown Size, Signature or Date, Circa 1879. Listed in the "Cleveland Herald" Dec. 15, 1879. (Same landscapes reflecting change in seasons.)

A-41 **Winter Sports**: (Missing): Oil: Unknown Size, Signature or Date, Circa 1881. (Dignified man caught in a snowball fight.)

A-42 **Shakers**: (Missing): Oil: Unknown Size, Signature or Date, Circa 1887. (Shaker family sitting in living room.)

A-43 **Going Home**: (Missing): Circa 1894.

A-44 **The Story of a Pumpkin Pie**: Book Illustration: Book by Wm. E. Barton, Pilgrim Press, Boston, 1898.

A-45 **Battle of Concord Bridge**: (Missing): Circa 1899.

A-46 **Dog & Parrot**: (Missing): Wm. Vischer. (Carpet in background.)

A-47 **Three Tramps**: (Missing): Oil: Byron Willard to Harry Willard to Evelyn Artz.

A-48 **The Scout**: (Missing): Water Color: 6″x-8″: Dr. Wm. Ridel, Cleveland, 1936. (Army scout in red shirt on plains with mountains in distance.)

A-49 **Night Fire Scene**: (Missing): Oil on Board: 18½″x12¼″: Not Signed or Dated: Ethel Quinlan, loaned to Willard Connally. No. 18 on back of canvas or frame. (Group of people at fire.)

A-50 **Still Life—Fruit**: (Missing): Ethel Quinlan.

A-51a **Jim Bludso**: (Missing): Oil: Approx. 15″x15″: Signed "A. M. Willard": Not Dated, Circa 1878: Col. John Hay. (Willard modeled for Jim Bludso, riverboat captain who stayed at wheel of burning ship.)

A-51b **Jim Bludso**: (Missing): Circa 1898: Copy for Wm. Walter Phelps.

A-52 **Barbara Fritchie**: (Missing): Lithograph: 18″x24″: Cleveland 1965.

A-53 **Scene on the Mississippi**: Lithograph: Size Unknown: Signed "A.M.W.": Published by W. J. Morgan Co., 1878: Library of Congress No. USZ62-8755. (Negro dock workers during work break.)

A-54 **The Danites**: Lithograph: 20″x27″: Signed "AM Willard": Published by W. J. Morgan & Co., No Date. (Two-panel study of lone woman in mining camp surrounded by men. No. 1 "Married, Mum?"; No. 2 "No, Sir!"): Library of Congress No. USZ62-8894: Bedford Hist. Soc.

A-55 **When in the Course of Human Events it Becomes Necessary**: Lithograph: (First in set of two): 23″x17″: Signed "A. M. Willard": Published by J. F. Ryder, No Date: Library of Congress, Bedford Historical Society. (American eagle and British lion squared off for battle in 1776.)

A-56 **Why Bless My Heart, Johnny, You're Welcome! How's Your Mother?**: Lithograph: (Second in set of two): 23″x17″: Signed "A. M. Willard": Published by J. F. Ryder, No Date: Library of Congress No. USZ62-11130. Bedford Historical Society. (Lion and eagle hooked to same carriage, as Uncle Sam welcomes British boy to Centennial in 1876.)

A-57 **United We Stand, Divided We Fall**: Lithograph: Size Unknown: Signed "A. M. Willard": Published by J. F. Ryder in 1875: Library of Congress No. USZ62-12331. (Two-panel study—No. 1, Two chickens in tog-of-war with worm; No. 2, Worm breaks and chickens fall over—other barnyard animals scatter.)

A-58 Ole Olson—Let Me See Your Tongue: Book Illustration: Size Unknown: Signed "A. M. Willard": Book by Gus Heege, Published by Shober & Carqueville, Chicago 1890. Library of Congress No. USZ62-15354: (Doctor examines young boy in highchair who is sticking out his tongue.)

A-59 Ole Olson—One Year Over: Book Illustration: Size Unknown: Signed "Willard": Book by Gus Heege, Published by Shober & Carqueville, Chicago: Not Dated, Circa 1890: Library of Congress No. USZ62-1030: (Well-dressed man).

A-60 Haf You Seen Ole Olson?: Book Illustration: Size Unknown: Signed "A. M. Willard": Book by Gus Heege, Published by Shober & Carqueville, Chicago, 1890. Library of Congress. (Two poorly-dressed men view laughing faces through holes in "Os" in title board.)

A-61 Uncle Tom's Cabin: Lithograph: 25"x-20": Signed "A. M. Willard": Published by Morgan Lithograph Co., Cleveland. Bedford Historical Society.

A-62 Minstel Show: Lithograph: 26"x21": Signed "A. Willard": Published by Morgan Lithograph Co., Cleveland: Bedford Historical Society.

A-63 Mrs. Grundy: Lithograph: 4¼"x6½": Signed "A. M. Willard": H.M.L. (Two women gossip over the gate while baby sits on the ground crying, with puppy chewing on his foot.)

A-64 Our First Parents—Before the Fall: Lithograph: 4¼"x6½": Not Signed or Dated: H.M.L. (First of pair) (Boy holds ladder with young girl on top who is reaching for apple.)

A-65 And After (Second of pair): Lithograph: 4¼"x6½": Not Signed: H.M.L. (Girl falls off ladder.)

A-66 That Husband of Mine: Lithograph: 4¼"x6½": Not Signed: H.M.L.

A-67 Thomas Concert: Lithograph: 4¼"x6½": Not Signed: H.M.L. (Cats on a roof—one is directing with a baton while others fight and howl.)

A-68 Contentment is Better Than Riches: Lithograph: 4¼"x6½": Not Signed: H.M.L. (Cleaning lady relaxes in chair fanning herself while lady of house looks on from behind.)

A-69 An Ounce of Prevention is Worth a Pound of Cure: Lithograph: 4¼"x6½": Signed "AM Willard": H.M.L. Published by J. F. Ryder, Cleveland. (Mother gives three children spoon of medicine.)

A-70 The Giddy Plumber: Lithograph: 4¼"x-6½": Not Signed or Dated: H.M.L.: Published by J. F. Ryder, Cleveland. (Plumber kisses cook in kitchen.) "All the afternoon he soft-shouldered the cook, then seventeen dollars he charged in his book."

A-71 Coming Events Cast Their Shadow Before: Lithograph: 4¼"x6½": Not Signed: Published by J. F. Ryder, Cleveland: H.M.L. (Children sit in pantry eating jam, while mother's shadow looms in background.)

A-72 A Stitch in Time Saves Nine: Lithograph: 4¼"x6½": Signed "A. M. Willard": Published by J. F. Ryder, Cleveland: H.M.L. (Mother, with son turned over her knee, sews up seat of his pants.)

A-73 A Hog Bite: Lithograph: 4¼"x6½": Signed "Willard": Published by J. F. Ryder, Cleveland: H.M.L. (Big boy takes huge bite from apple, while smaller boy tries to take it back.)

A-74 Prepare to Pucker: Lithograph: 4¼"x-6½": Not Signed or Dated: Published by J. F. Ryder, Cleveland: H.M.L. (Five girls trying to whistle, while laughing.)

A-75 Many a Slip Twixt Cup & Lip (First of Pair): Lithograph: 4¼"x6½": Not Signed: Published by J. F. Ryder, Cleveland: H.M.L. (Farmer leans precariously over to drink from stream, while a ram eyes him from behind.)

A-76 Many a Slip Twixt Cup & Lip (Second of Pair): Lithograph: 4¼"x6½": Not Signed: Published by J. F. Ryder, Cleveland: H.M.L. (Farmer, having been butted into the water, stands dripping, while he and the ram glare at each other.)

A-77 My Grandfather's Clock: Lithograph: 4¼"x6½": Not Signed: Published by J. F. Ryder, Cleveland: H.M.L. (Cat tied to swinging clock pendulum by tail; boy and dog look on.)

A-78 Cornelia's Jewels: (Missing): Water Color: (Small): Mrs. Max Cook.

A-79 Grandma's Chair: Sketch in Book: 8''x-10'': Signed "A. M. Willard": Not Dated, Circa 1883: Printed in "The Sketch Book," Cleveland Public Library. (Young girl with doll in rocking chair.)

A-80 Views in the Holy Land of Chautauqua: Sketch in Book: 8''x10'': Not Signed or Dated, Circa 1883: Printed in "The Sketch Book," Cleveland Public Library. (Caricature of friends during artist's outing to lake.)

A-81 Impish Boy: Sketch in Book: 6''x8'': Signed "Willard": Not Dated, Circa 1883: Printed in "The Sketch Book," Cleveland Public Library. (Boy sitting on stool, sticking tongue out.)

A-82 The Old Shaker Mill: Sketch in Book: 8''x-10'': Signed "Willard": Not Dated, Circa 1883: Printed in "The Sketch Book", Cleveland Public Library. (View of mill and trees.)

A-83 Study of Cow & Sheep: Sketch in Book: 8''x10'': Signed "A.M.W.": Not Dated, Circa 1883: Printed in "The Sketch Book," Cleveland Public Library. (Cow and two sheep.)

A-84 Canal Lock: Sketch in Book: 8''x10'': Signed "A.M.W.": Not Dated, Circa 1883: Printed in "The Sketch Book," Cleveland Public Library. (Canal lock with open gate, houses in background.)

A-85 Barton's Ancestor: Oil: Unknown Size, Signature or Date: Photo at H.M.L. (Barton knocks British officer with sword from horse by hitting him with bucket.)

A-86 Ouch: (Missing)

A-87 Before the Boom (First of Pair): (Missing)

A-88 After the Boom (Second of Pair): (Missing)

A-89 View of the Southern Mississippi: (Missing): Oil: Unknown Size, Signature or Date, Circa 1881. (Steamboat in river, family under tree left, cotton pickers right.)

A-90 What Are the Wild Waves Saying, Brother? (First of Pair): (Missing)

A-91 Scoot, Brother, Scoot (Second of Pair): (Missing)

A-92 Primitive Dentistry: Oil: 30''x24'': Circa 1875: Dr. Martin J. Noble to Homer C. Noble to Martin J. Noble to Allen J. Noble to Mrs. Judith Weir. (Village blacksmiths extracting tooth from farmer, who is supporting himself crab-fashion on the floor. Outside stands a horse with a tear-drop in his eye.)

A-93 Village of Wellington: Oil: 35''x27'': Signed and Dated, "A. M. Willard/1857": Mary Cady to Wil Tossot to H.M.L. (Wellington scene with buildings, figures, and horses and carriages.)

A-94 Pioneer with Gun: (Missing): Oil: (Medium Size): Signed "A.M.W.": Not Dated. (Pioneer carrying gun over shoulder—walking through forest.)

A-95a Bone of Contention: Lithograph: (Pair): 15½''x22½'': Signed "A. M. Willard": Not Dated or Publisher Listed: H.M.L.: (No. 1—Two boys in cart hang on as dog that is pulling cart is chasing another dog with bone. No. 2—Cart is smashed as one boy stands crying, while other boy tries to separate dog fight.) (Variation of Pluck theme.)

A-95b Bone of Contention: Oil: "Smith," 1976.

A-95c Bone of Contention: I. M. Fitzsimmons

PLUCK

PL-1 (Cat) I. Oil: 25''x16½'': Not Signed or Dated: L. H. Norton to W.R.H.S.: W.R.H.S. No. 40.82.

II. Same: W.R.H.S. No. 40.83.

PL-2 (Rabbit) I. Oil: 16''x12'': Signed "A. M. Willard": Not Dated: Stouffer Foods Corp. to Willard F. Gordon.

II. Same: Stolen from Stouffer Foods Corp., Washington, D.C., 1960's.

PL-3 (Rabbit) I. Oil, Sepia: 20''x15½'': Not Signed or Dated: Hunkin to W.R.H.S.: W.H.R.S. No. 1930-1.

II. Same: W.R.H.S. No. 1930-2.

PL-4 (Rabbit) I. Oil: 30''x24'': Not Signed or Dated: H. T. Clark to W.R.H.S.: W.H.R.S. No. 1945.

II. Missing.

PL-5 I. Missing: James Brennan, 1936.

II. Same.

PL-6 I. Missing: Mrs. Byron Willard, 1936.
II. Same.

PL-7 (Rabbit) I. Missing: Advertisement, Liberty Mutual Life Ins. Co.
II. Missing: No Photo available.

PL-8 (Rabbit) I. Lithograph: Unknown Size: Signed "A. M. Willard": Overprinted "Ent Acc to Act of Congress the year 1872 by A. M. Willard in the Dept of the Libr of Cong at Wash DC" and "Published by J. F. Ryder, Cleveland": Library of Congress No. USZ62-11132.
II. Same: Library of Congress No. USZ62-11131.

PL-9 (Rabbit) I. Oil: 30″x23″: Signed "WILLARD": Not Dated: Inscription, "Painted for Addie Tripp": H.M.L. **II.** Missing.

PL-10 I. Missing: Wodsworth to F. E. Wiles.
II. Same.

PL-11 I. Oil: 30″x22″: Not Signed or Dated: K. L. Barker. **II.** Missing.

PL-12 I. Unknown: Mrs. Donald Metzger.
II. Unknown.

PL-13 I. Unknown.: Curtis to John Thomas to Ann C. Graff. **II.** Same.

PL-14 (Rabbit) I. Missing: Oil: 22″ x 29″
II. Oil: 22″ x 29″, Unknown Signature or Date: Janetta Evins.

PL-15 I & II. Oil: Cherlyn Yost Hathaway.

PORTRAITS

P-1 Self Portrait I: Oil: 22″x27″: Not Signed or Dated, Circa 1865: Roxbury Historical Society to Abbot Hall, Marblehead.

P-2 Self Portrait II: Oil: 23″x28″: Not Signed or Dated, Circa 1876: Alfred Willard to W.R.H.S.: No. 41.1374.

P-3 Self Portrait III: Oil: 23″x28″: Not Signed or Dated, Circa 1900: Margo Willard to Alfred Willard to W.R.H.S.: W.R.H.S. No. 61.36.

P-4 Eniolus Willard: Oil: 26″x30″: Not Signed or Dated, Circa 1860. (Nephew of artist (1852-1857). May have been painted after his death.): F. W. Bottemus to Geauga County Historical Society, Burton, Ohio.

P-5 Tripp Girls: Oil: 41½″x44½″: Not Signed or Dated, Circa 1865: Mrs. Wm. Hemenway to Mrs. Sidney T. Hemenway to H.M.L. (Addie Tripp [Hemenway] left, and Carrie Tripp [Vischer] right.)

P-6 Emma Bennett Noble I: Oil: 28″x34″: Signed "A. M. Willard": Not Dated, Circa 1870: Emma Bennett Noble to Harry S. Bennett to Edward S. Wells.

P-7 Emma Bennett Noble II: Oil:

P-8 Emma Annette Howk: Oil: John Howk to Clara Disbro.

P-9 Hattie Adel Pratt: ("Blue Girl"): Oil: 27½″x39½″: Not Signed or Dated, Circa 1865. Burton Pratt to H.M.L. (Died 1862 at three years of age. Portrait painted from small photograph.)

P-10 Hattie: Oil: 35″x36¼″: Not Signed or Dated, Circa 1870's: F. J. Arnold.

P-11 Reverend Samuel R. Willard I (Father): Oil: 26″x31″: Not Signed or Dated, Circa 1865: V. L. Merriman to Geauga Co. Hist. Soc., Burton, Ohio.

P-12 Reverend Samuel R. Willard II (Father): Oil: 22″x27″: Not Signed or Dated, Circa 1870: T. A. Willard to Verna Willard Clifford to Willard F. Gordon.

P-13 Catherine Willard (Mother): Oil: 22″x-27″: Not Signed or Dated, Circa 1870: T. A. Willard to Verna Willard Clifford to Willard F. Gordon.

P-14 Maude Connally (Daughter): (Missing): Oil: Ethel Quinlan, Cleveland, 1936.

P-15 Brother (?): (Missing): Oil: Ethel Quinlan, Cleveland, 1936.

P-16 Son (?): (Missing): Oil: Ethel Quinlan, Cleveland, 1936.

P-17 Harry Willard (Son): Oil: Margo Willard to Elayne Bylund to Alden Hare.

P-18 Eliza Jane Adams: Oil: 22″x27″ Oval: Not Signed or Dated, Circa 1867: Jane Trotter Adams to Eliza Jane Adams to Winifred Park.

P-19 Everett Morton Gott I: 26″x32″: Pastel Chalk: Not Signed or Dated, Circa 1885: Ella Adel Adams Gott to Winifred Park to Willard F. Gordon.

P-20 Evetett Morton Gott II: 14½″x18″: Water Color: Not Signed or Dated, Circa 1887: Ella Adel Adams Gott to Winifred Park.

P-21 Miriam Miller: Oil: 17″x21″: Not Signed or Dated: W.R.H.S. No. 49.501.

P-22 Boy: (Son?): Oil: (Missing): Stouffer Food Corp., Cleveland.

P-23 Isaac Bruce Read: Oil: 23″x26″: Signed and Dated, "A. M. Willard/1912": Evelyn Jenne to W.R.H.S.: W.R.H.S. No. 62.69.2.

P-24 Woman in Dancing Position: Pastel: 26″x37″: Not Signed or Dated: W.R.H.S. No. 49.805

P-25 Shaker Elder of North Union Village: Oil: 27″x37″: Not Signed or Dated, Circa 1887: Willard Estate to W.R.H.S.: W.R.H.S. No. 41.1891

P-26 Frank Bennett: Oil: 23″x27″: Signed "A. Willard": Not Dated, Circa 1863: P. D. Lattimer.

P-27 Hugh Mosher: (Missing): Probably Water Color: Size Unknown: Signed "A. M. Willard": Inscribed "Original sketch of fifer in Yankee Doodle Hugh Mosher 1876": Photo at H.M.L.

P-28 Head of Hugh Mosher: (Missing): Oil: Seen in Cleveland in 1960's.

P-29 Detail of Fifer: (Missing): H.M.L. Exhibition 1955, Dr. B. Colver.

P-30 Boy: Water Color: 15½″x22″: Not Signed or Dated, Circa 1880's: Edward S. Wells.

P-31 Rollin Dellaraine Foote: Oil: 19½″x24″: Not Signed or Dated, Circa 1877: R. D. Foote to Keith Andrews.

P-32 General Garfield: Oil: Unknown Size, Signature or Date, Circa 1881: (At Chickamauga)

P-33 Hugh Mosher: Oil: 24″x46″: Signed "A. M. Willard": Not Dated, Circa 1890: R. A. Demery to H.M.L.

P-34 Head of St. Paul: (Missing): Oil on Leather: Dr. Richardson, 1936.

P-35 Young Girl: Pencil Sketch: 4″x5″: Signed "A. M. Willard": Not Dated, Circa 1879. W. H. Eckman Scrap Book, W.R.H.S. Manuscript MSS No. 820.

P-36 Mrs. Edwards: (Missing): Oil: Mrs. Geo. Richardson, 1936.

P-37 Old Man—Shaker: (Missing): Oil: 30″x-37″: Unknown Signature, Not Dated, Circa 1887: Cleveland School of Art.

P-38 Mr. Townsend: (Missing): Charcoal: 24″x30″ Oval: Unknown Signature or Date: Robert Townsend, 1936.

P-39 Mr. Bennett: (Missing): Oil: Roy Bennett.

P-40 Minnie Willard (Niece): Oil: 26½″x39″: Not Signed or Dated, Circa 1860's: Dr. John Wherry.

P-41 Harvey L. Carey: Oil: 24″x29″ Oval: Not Signed or Dated: Edgar P. Weber to W.R.H.S.: W.R.H.S. No. 67.105.2

P-42 Jane Russell Carey: Oil: 24″x29″ Oval: Not Signed or Dated: Edgar P. Weber to W.R.H.S.: W.R.H.S. No. 67.105.1

P-43 Old Man With White Beard and Cane: Unknown: Photo at H.M.L.

P-44 John Hay: Unknown

LANDSCAPES

L-1 Oil: 14″x21″: Signed "A. M. Willard": Not Dated: Willard Estate to Alfred R. Willard, Borrowed by Alden Hare: (Woods, small stream center.)

L-2 Oil: 21″x14″: Signed "A. M. Willard": Not Dated: Ethel Quinlan to W.R.H.S.: W.R.H.S. No. 2808: (#3 marked on back of frame): (Sheep center, hill right with burnt tree stumps.)

L-3 Oil: 36″x20″: Signed "A. M. Willard": Not Dated: J. B. Read to Evelyn Jenne to W.R.H.S.: W.R.H.S. No. 62.69.1: (Stream and cattle left—large tree right.)

L-4 Oil: 20''x14'': Signed "A. M. Willard": Not Dated: Mrs. Gilbert Schafer to W.R.H.S.: W.R.H.S. No. 62.149.4: (Chagrin River, falls, town in center.)

L-5 Oil: 20''x14'': Signed "A. M. Willard": Not Dated: Ethel Quinlan to W.R.H.S.: W.R.H.S. No. 2807: (Wood scene, with fallen tree in foreground) (#19 marked on back of frame).

L-6 Oil on Board: 18½''x12¼'': Not Signed or Dated: Ethel Quinlan to W.R.H.S.: W.R.H.S. No. 42.122: (#14 marked on back). (River scene, with palisades, lighthouse on top).

L-7 Oil on Board: (Painted both sides—L-8 painted on other side of board): 18½''x12¼'': Not Signed or Dated: Ethel Quinlan to W.R.H.S.: W.R.H.S. No. 42.125: (#16 marked on edge): (Stream right, group of old buildings left).

L-8 Oil on Board: (Painted both sides—L-7 painted on other side of board): 18½''x12¼'': Not Signed or Dated: Ethel Quinlan to W.R.H.S.: W.R.H.S. No. 42.125: (#16 marked on edge): (Stream, with rail fence left, two houses in distance).

L-9 Oil on Board: 18½''x12¼'': Not Signed or Dated: Ethel Quinlan to W.R.H.S.: W.R.H.S. No. 42.123: (#15 on back): (Fall scene, river in foreground, piece of old fence at right).

L-10 Oil on Board: 18½''x12¼'': Signed "A. M. Willard": Not Dated: Ethel Quinlan to W.R.H.S.: W.R.H.S. No. 42.124: (#13 on back): (Fall scene with rail fence at left).

L-11 Oil: 20''x14'': Signed "A. M. Willard": Not Dated: Ethel Quinlan to W.R.H.S.: W.R.H.S. No. 42.118: (River foreground, rocks and pine trees background).

L-12 Oil: 20''x14'': Signed "A. M. Willard": Not Dated: Ethel Quinlan to W.R.H.S.: W.R.H.S. No. 42.119: (#2 on back of frame): (River scene at Taylor's Falls on St. Croyx).

L-13 Oil: 22''x16'': Not Signed or Dated: Ethel Quinlan to W.R.H.S.: W.R.H.S. No. 42.120: (#5 on back of frame): (Woodland scene, brook center, meadow right).

L-14 Oil: 30''x20'': Not Signed or Dated: Ethel Quinlan to W.R.H.S.: W.R.H.S. No. 42.126: (22 on back of frame): (Farm scene with pond at right).

L-15 (Missing): Oil: Ada Pierce Read to Evelyn Jenne: (Ashtabula Valley).

L-16 **Grand Canyon**: Oil: 20½''x15½'': Signed "A. M. Willard": Not Dated: Ethel Quinlan to W.R.H.S.: W.R.H.S. No. 2804: (#20 on back of frame).

L-17 **Grand Canyon**: Oil: 15½''x20½'': Not Signed or Dated: Ethel Quinlan to W.R.H.S.: W.R.H.S. No. 2805: (#21 on back of frame).

L-18 Oil: 20½''x14½'': Not Signed or Dated: Ethel Quinlan to W.R.H.S.: W.R.H.S. No. 2806: (#1 on back of frame): (River scene, two cows in foreground).

L-19 Oil: 19''x12½'': Not Signed or Dated: Ethel Quinlan to W.R.H.S.: W.R.H.S. No. 2809: (#8 marked on back of frame): (Lake scene, shoreline with sand dune lower right).

L-20 Oil: 39''x35'': Not Signed or Dated: Mrs. Wm. Rose to W.R.H.S.: W.R.H.S. No. 42.185: (Mountains in background, lake and stream at foot of mountains, cattle at side of lake, goats grazing on hillside).

L-21 Oil: 20''x14'': Signed and Dated, "A. M. Willard/1882'': C. G. Vernooy: (Cattle foreground, lake center, house and trees background).

L-22 Oil: 24½''x26'': Not Signed or Dated: Wm. McCloskey to Geauga Co. Historical Society, Burton, Ohio: (Rock left, on which two figures stand. Mountain background, horse and rider in center).

L-23 **Ashtabula Valley**: (Missing)

L-24 **Black River**: (Missing)

L-25 Water Color: 14''x11'': Signed "A. M. Willard": Not Dated: Evelyn Jenne to Edward S. Wells: (Rural scene, brook, trees and small bridge center).

L-26 Oil: 12½''x19½'': Signed "A.M.W.": Not Dated: Winifred A. Park: (Stream bottom, snow capped mountain top).

L-27 Oil: 12½''x19½'': Signed "A. M. Willard": Not Dated: Maud Willard to Mrs. Bert (Mary L.) Graves: (Pond center and left, fence back center, building on right).

L-28 Southern Scene: (Missing)

L-29 Wayside Landscape: (Missing): Small: A. Fisher to Rev. H. H. Fisher to Ernest Root.

L-30 Landscape of a Creek: (Missing): 12"x-16": Kenneth Sifert, 1936.

L-31 Old Mill Dam & Mill: (Missing): Water Color: 10"x14": Kenneth Sifert, 1936.

L-32 Valley of Aurora Branch Chagrin River: (Missing): Oil: Circa 1900: C. A. Rock, Cleveland, 1936.

L-33 Rural Farm Scene: (Missing): Oil: 36"x-24": Circa 1872: Henry D. Parsons, 1936.

L-34 Sunset on Mt. Baldi: (Missing): Water Color: Circa 1896: Clarence J. Willard, 1936.

L-35 Prova Canyon: (Missing): Oil: 12¼"x-18½": Not Signed: Unknown if Dated: Ethel Quinlan, borrowed by Willard Connally: (#6 on back).

L-36 (Missing): Oil: 11¼"x18½": Not Signed: Unknown if Dated: Ethel Quinlan, borrowed by Willard Connally: (#7 on back): (Rural scene, bridge to left, cottage to center and right).

L-37 (Missing): Oil: 12¼"x18½": Signed, but Unknown Where or How: Not Dated: Ethel Quinlan, borrowed by Willard Connally: (#9 on back): (Forest scene, fallen tree at right).

L-38 (Missing): Oil: 12¼"x18½": Not Signed: Unknown if Dated: Ethel Quinlan, borrowed by Willard Connally: (#10 on back): (Tropical scene, palm trees).

L-39 (Missing): Oil: 12¼"x18½": Not Signed: Unknown if Dated: Ethel Quinlan, borrowed by Willard Connally: (#11 on back): (Rural scene with road and bridge across stream).

L-40 (Missing): Oil: 12¼"x18½": Signed, but Unknown Where or How: Unknown if Dated: Ethel Quinlan, borrowed by Willard Connally: (#12 on back): (Fall scene showing trees on bank in background).

L-41 (Missing): Oil: 12¼"x18½": Not Signed: Unknown if Dated: Ethel Quinlan, borrowed by Willard Connally: (#17 on back): (Tree in center).

L-42 Sea & Cliff: Water Color: 15"x5": Signed "A.M.W.": Not Dated: Mrs. Carl Woodin to H.M.L.

L-43 Unknown Medium: 14"x20": Signed, but Unknown Where or How: Unknown if Dated: Mrs. Burton Maxwell.

L-44 Oil: 20"x14": Signed "A. M. Willard": Unknown if Dated: John C. Wherry to H.M.L.: (Creek left, mill right, fence and meadow center).

L-45 Oil: 15"x10": Signed "A. M. Willard": Not Dated: John C. Wherry to H.M.L.: (Creek left, road and large trees right).

L-46 Oil: 20"x14": Signed "A. M. Willard": Not Dated: Emma P. Colver to H.M.L.: (Creek bottom, large trees and fence left).

L-47 Oil: 20"x14": Signed "A. M. Willard": Not Dated: Anne Colver Graff to H.M.L.: (River scene; falls center, house right, town top center).

L-48 Chagrin Valley Scene: Oil: 20"x14": Signed "A. M. Willard": Not Dated: Anne Colver Graff to H.M.L.: (Wheat shocks in field).

L-49 Mountain Scene: Oil: 33"x22": Signed and Dated, "A. M. Willard/1918": Inscription on back, "Last known painting": Anne Colver Graff to H.M.L.: (Mountains background, grape field foreground, farm buildings right).

L-50 Provo Canyon—Bald Mt. Utah: Oil: 28"x-21": Signed "A. M. Willard": Not Dated: Anne Colver Graff to H.M.L.: (Mountains background and left, stream center, and trees right).

L-51 Old Mill: Oil: 12"x18": Not Signed or Dated: Anne Colver Graff to H.M.L.: (Mill top center, falls right, rocks bottom).

L-52 Oil: 20"x14": Signed "A.M.W.": Not Dated: Mrs. Marian Stombaugh: (Stream left, with flowering bushes right and picnic group center).

L-53 Seascape: (Missing): Water Color: Margo Willard to Evelyn Artz.

L-54 Landscape: (Missing): Artz Estate to Mrs. Rivers to Paul Rivers.

L-55 Landscape: (Missing): A. C. Pohlman to "Spirit of '76" Post #8 American Legion.

L-56 Seascape: (Missing): Wodsworth to F. E. Wiles to Mrs. Betty Wagner: (Sailboat on water): (Back inscribed, "Painted by A. M. Willard").

L-57 Landscape: (Two in oval frame): (Missing): Wodsworth to F. E. Wiles, 1955.

L-58 Sketches of Florida Coast: (Missing): Circa 1897.

L-59 Woodland Scene: Oil: Signed "A.M.W.": Boyd McConnell: (Hunter in a forest).

MURALS

M-1 Spirit of U. S. MAIL: Oil on Plaster: 10'x-14': Signed "A. M. WILL-" on letter: Circa 1882-1885: Washington Court House, Fayette Co., Ohio.

M-2 Spirit of Telegraph: Oil on Plaster: 10'x-14': Not Signed or Dated, Circa 1882-1885: Washington Court House, Fayette Co., Ohio.

M-3 Spirit of Electricity: Oil on Plaster: 10'x-14': Not Signed or Dated, Circa 1882-1885: Washington Court House, Fayette Co., Ohio.

M-4 Girl With Fruit Basket: Oil on Plaster: 18½''x66'': Not Dated, Circa 1880's: S.L.C.H.S.

M-5 Soldier in Armor with Spear: Oil on Plaster: 18½''x66'': Not Signed or Dated, Circa 1880's: S.L.C.H.S.

M-6 Moore House: Oil on Plaster: Circa 1882-1885: Miss Marion Moore, Washington Court House, Ohio. (Numerous vignettes on walls and ceiling. Flags with shield and eagle over fireplace, Restorations by Miss Moore.

SCULPTURE

SC-1 General Garfield: (Missing): Clay: Circa 1881

SC-2 Spirit of '76 Trio: (Missing): Wood

SC-3 Old Drummer: (Missing): Clay